THE YEAR OF THE
BRUINS

Library and Archives Canada Cataloguing in Publication data available upon request.

NHL, the NHL Shield and the word mark and image of the Stanley Cup are registered trademarks of the National Hockey League. All NHL logos and marks and NHL team logos and marks depicted herein are the property of the NHL and the respective teams and may not be reproduced without the prior written consent of NHL Enterprises, L.P. NHL 2011. All Rights Reserved.

We acknowledge the financial support of the Government of Canada through the Book Publishing Industry Development Program and that of the Government of Ontario through the Ontario Media Development Corporation's Ontario Book Initiative. We further acknowledge the support of the Canada Council for the Arts and the Ontario Arts Council for our publishing program.

Published simultaneously in the United States of America by McClelland & Stewart Ltd., P.O. Box 1030, Plattsburgh, New York 12901

Library of Congress Control Number: 2011931815

Designed by First Image
Printed and bound in the United States of America

All photographs copyright NHL/Getty Images

FENN / McClelland & Stewart Ltd.
75 Sherbourne Street
Toronto, Ontario
M5A 2P9
www.mcclelland.com

The Official Publication of the 2011 Stanley Cup Final

THE YEAR OF THE
BRUINS

Celebrating Boston's 2010-11 Stanley Cup Championship Season

2011 STANLEY CUP CHAMPIONS

OFFICIAL LICENSED PRODUCT · PRODUIT LICENCIÉ OFFICIEL

Andrew Podnieks

FENN
M&S

CONTENTS

Conference Final

Boston vs. Tampa Bay

Boston wins best-of-seven 4-3

Stanley Cup Final

Boston vs. Vancouver

Boston wins best-of-seven 4-3

Team History

Player Biographies

INTRODUCTION

The 2010 playoffs could not have ended more horribly for the Bruins. After beating Buffalo in six games to start the post-season, they won the first three games against the Flyers only to lose the next four. Worse, they led game seven 3–0 and lost 4–3. This was hardly the best way to start the next season, 2010–11, coming after this nightmare finish, but general manager Peter Chiarelli, coach Claude Julien, and captain Zdeno Chara didn't panic.

Indeed, Chiarelli made not a single significant free agent signing last summer. He did, though, make several key trades over the course of the year that pushed the talent-laden Bruins to the top. A solid playoff team became a top playoff contender. And then, of course, the Tim Thomas Factor was added to the mix.

At the 2010 draft Chiarelli acquired Nathan Horton and Gregory Campbell from the Florida Panthers for Dennis Wideman and two draft choices. Horton was under-valued in Florida but quickly proved his worth as a star forward who could score and make significant contributions to the offence and, tangentially, to the dressing room.

Then, as the trade deadline approached, the GM made three other deals. First, he acquired Tomas Kaberle from Toronto. Kaberle was a steady defenceman who moved the puck out of his own end without panicking and with consistent success. Chiarelli also got Chris Kelly from Ottawa and Rich Peverley from Atlanta, role players who proved invaluable during the marathon that is the playoffs.

Lastly, he signed free agent Shane Hnidy, who slowly worked his way into the lineup after all other twenty-nine teams had passed on a chance to sign him.

But the core of the team remained intact from that horrible 2010 playoff experience. From Chara, the captain, to forty-two-year-old Mark Recchi, to Patrice Bergeron, and to Michael Ryder, they were all back for 2010–11. At a time many a GM might have pointed the blame finger at his top stars, Chiarelli gave them all a vote of confidence.

Added to the mix came second-overall draft choice Tyler Seguin and young star Milan Lucic, who both had great seasons and showed Boston fans how bright was the team's future. And then there was goalie Tim Thomas. He reminds one of Jarome Iginla, for no matter how grave the game moment or serious the team situation, Thomas wears a smile on his face with a joy that resonates. He knows how lucky he is to be playing hockey for a living. He knows how fun the game is. He knows, too, that he can be the best.

Thomas was nothing short of sensational during the regular season, helping the Bruins to first place in the Northeast Division with 103 points. But the team started the 2011 playoffs in a way that suggested more disaster was on the immediate horizon. They lost their first two home games to Montreal, a team that had won twenty-four of thirty-two series over the years between the teams, and headed to the Bell Centre with many people talking sweep for the Canadiens.

But the Bruins proved they had learned from 2010. They won the next two games in the hostile environs of Montreal, and eliminated the Habs in seven games. Thomas played well in goal, and the team was building momentum.

That momentum grew by leaps and bounds when they won the first two games of the next series in Philadelphia, and then came home and swept the Flyers, earning a week's rest and proving they were a Stanley Cup contender. Their incredible seven-game battle with Tampa Bay put them in the final, and Thomas was now playing lights-out hockey in goal, truly giving his team a chance to win every night.

His play got better in the Stanley Cup Final. Although the Bruins lost three close games in Vancouver, he was the best player on either side. The Bruins won all three games in Boston, and Thomas was virtually unbeatable. Game seven, in Vancouver, was a defining moment for him, and he responded. So, too, did Patrice Bergeron, who scored twice including a game-turning short-handed goal late in the second period to give the Bruins a 3–0 lead. They went on to win, 4–0, taking home the Stanley Cup for the first time in thirty-nine years.

This was not a realistic scenario a year ago as they were shaking hands with the Flyers, but they persevered. And that's what winning the Stanley Cup is all about.

Slovakia's Zdeno Chara becomes just the second European captain to win the Stanley Cup after Nicklas Lidstrom (Sweden) won with Detroit in 2008.

THE BIRTH OF THE BOSTON BRUINS

On November 1, 1924, Charles Adams realized a dream when the NHL granted him the first franchise in the United States. Adams hired Art Ross as the team's general manager, and he named the team the Bruins because of its association with ruggedness. He chose the colours brown and yellow for the team because these were the colours used by his chain of grocery stores, called First National Stores.

The Bruins played their first game on December 1, 1924, beating the Montreal Maroons, 2–1, at the Boston Arena. The team made its first push to greatness two years later, when Ross managed to sign Eddie Shore, who would soon become one of the greatest defencemen in the game. The Bruins made it to the Stanley Cup Final in Shore's first year and won it all just two years later with a roster that also included goalie Tiny Thompson and Dit Clapper.

But it was the years just before World War Two that were Boston's finest. The team won the Stanley Cup in 1939, and again in 1941, and was led by the Kraut Line of Woody Dumart, Bobby Bauer, and Milt Schmidt, three childhood friends from Kitchener, Ontario (formerly Berlin before World War One). Although the team. Although the team continued to make the playoffs regularly after the war, great success was still a long way off.

The team missed the playoffs for eight straight years (1959–67), but the last of those was the first with an eighteen-year-old named Bobby Orr on the blue-line. The Bruins made the playoffs a record twenty-nine times in a row thereafter, winning the Cup in 1970 and 1972 with some of the greatest players ever. The Big, Bad Bruins had Orr on defence, Phil Esposito, Ken Hodge, and Wayne Cashman as the top-scoring line, and goalie Gerry Cheevers. It was also one of the toughest teams and never backed down or was intimidated.

After Orr, it was Ray Bourque who was the star player on the team, but he was never able to bring the Bruins a Stanley Cup victory. Despite many great players over the more recent years, the 1972 Cup win was still the team's last before this magical ride in 2011.

Bobby Orr was the greatest Bruins defenceman of all time, combining grace and power with a competitive spirit unmatched in the game.

BOSTON GARDEN AND TD GARDEN

The Boston Garden opened on November 17, 1928, and served as the home of the Bruins for nearly seven decades. Built by Tex Rickard, the team played its first game on November 20, 1928, losing 1–0 to the Montreal Canadiens.

Because Rickard built it with boxing in mind, and because there were no rules for rink dimensions, the Garden was actually nearly ten feet shorter and two feet narrower than the standard NHL rink of 200 by 85 feet. As a result, it was one of the most difficult and intimidating buildings for visiting teams to play in.

As time passed, though, the Garden's charms became its flaws, and the small capacity (15,000), lack of air conditioning, absence of luxury boxes, and the steel beams which obstructed views, all highlighted the need for a modern arena. In October 1995, the new Fleet Center opened (later renamed TD Garden) and two years later the original Garden was demolished.

The Bruins were founded in 1924 and for their first four years played out of the Boston Arena. It still exists under the name Matthews Arena. Located near Northeastern University, it opened in 1910.

Boston has had one of the most successful teams in NHL history since it joined the league in 1924.

In his four years with the Bruins, and eight coaching in the NHL, Julien has earned his stripes the hard way, through experience and putting in the time. As a player, he had played in the OHA with Oshawa and Windsor before spending five years in the minors in the hopes of making the NHL. In 1984, with the Quebec Nordiques, he did.

The burly defenceman played just fourteen games over two seasons, though, spending the next several years back in the minors. He retired as a player in 1992, and in 1996 became the coach of Hull in the QMJHL, winning the Memorial Cup in his first season. After five seasons he assumed the head coaching position with the Hamilton Bulldogs of the AHL, the farm team of the Montreal Canadiens. Three years later he realized his dream when the Habs hired him mid-season. The team missed the playoffs in his first year but qualified the next, but after the lockout he lasted only half a season before being fired.

Julien had no trouble finding a new job, landing in New Jersey under Lou Lamoriello, who was always partial to Habs coaches. Strangely, though, Lamroiello fired Julien with only three games left in the regular season and the team in first place in the division.

That summer he was hired by the Bruins and has been with the club ever since. In his second season the team won fifty-three games and he was named coach of the year, and the team made it to the second round of the playoffs in 2009 and again the next year.

Claude Julien is the first coach since Tom Johnson in 1972 to win the Bruins a Stanley Cup.

TRAINING CAMP ROSTER

Player	2010-11 Status
Yuri Alexandrov	played for Providence, AHL
Jamie Arniel	played for Providence, AHL
Matt Bartkowski	played for Providence, AHL
Patrice Bergeron	played for Boston, NHL
Andrew Bodnarchuk	played for Providence, AHL
Johnny Boychuk	played for Boston, NHL
Ryan Button	played in WHL & AHL
Gregory Campbell	played for Boston, NHL
Jordan Caron	played for Providence, AHL
Zdeno Chara	played for Boston, NHL
Joe Colborne	traded to Toronto, NHL
Adam Courchaine	played in ECHL
Craig Cunningham	played in WHL
Matt Dalton	played in AHL & ECHL
Matt Delahey	played in ECHL
Ryan Donald	played in AHL & ECHL
Andrew Ference	played for Boston, NHL
Alain Goulet	played in AHL & ECHL
Zach Hamill	played for Providence, AHL
Shane Hnidy	played for Boston, NHL
Nathan Horton	played for Boston, NHL
Matt Hunwick	traded to Colorado, NHL
Michael Hutchinson	played in AHL & ECHL
Steven Kampfer	played for Boston & Providence
Jordan Knackstedt	played in AHL
Jared Knight	played in OHL & AHL
David Krejci	played for Boston, NHL
Jeffrey LoVecchio	played in AHL
Milan Lucic	played for Boston, NHL
Lane MacDermid	played for Providence, AHL
Kirk MacDonald	played for Providence, AHL
Brad Marchand	played for Boston, NHL
Nathan McIver	played for Providence, AHL
Adam McQuaid	played for Boston, NHL
Levi Nelson	played in AHL
Daniel Paille	played for Boston, NHL
Jeff Penner	played for Providence, AHL
Tyler Randell	played in OHL
Tuukka Rask	played for Boston, NHL
Mark Recchi	played for Boston, NHL
Jeremy Reich	played for Providence, AHL
Yannick Riendeau	played in AHL & ECHL
Antoine Roussel	played in AHL & ECHL
Joe Rullier	played in ECHL
Michael Ryder	played for Boston, NHL
Max Sauve	played for Providence, AHL
Marc Savard	played for Boston, NHL
Nolan Schaefer	played for Providence, AHL
Tyler Seguin	played for Boston, NHL
Dennis Seidenberg	played for Boston, NHL
Wyatt Smith	played in AHL & DEL
Ryan Spooner	played in OHL
Mark Stuart	traded to Atlanta, NHL
Marco Sturm	released, played with Los Angeles & Washington, NHL
Tim Thomas	played for Boston, NHL
Shawn Thornton	played for Boston, NHL
Blake Wheeler	traded to Atlanta, NHL
Trent Whitfield	played for Providence, AHL
Cody Wild	played in AHL & ECHL
Walker Wintoneak	played in CHL & CIAU

Atlantic Division

	GP	W	L	OT	GF	GA	Pts
Philadelphia	82	47	23	12	259	223	106
Pittsburgh	82	49	25	8	238	199	106
NY Rangers	82	44	33	5	233	198	93
New Jersey	82	38	39	5	174	209	81
NY Islanders	82	30	39	13	229	264	73

Northeast Division

	GP	W	L	OT	GF	GA	Pts
Boston	82	46	25	11	246	195	103
Montreal	82	44	30	8	216	209	96
Buffalo	82	43	29	10	245	229	96
Toronto	82	37	34	11	218	251	85
Ottawa	82	32	40	10	192	250	74

Southeast Division

	GP	W	L	OT	GF	GA	Pts
Washington	82	48	23	11	224	197	107
Tampa Bay	82	46	25	11	247	240	103
Carolina	82	40	31	11	236	239	91
Atlanta	82	34	36	12	223	269	80
Florida	82	30	40	12	195	229	72

Central Division

	GP	W	L	OT	GF	GA	Pts
Detroit	82	47	25	10	261	241	104
Nashville	82	44	27	11	219	194	99
Chicago	82	44	29	9	258	225	97
St. Louis	82	38	33	11	240	234	87
Columbus	82	34	35	13	215	258	81

Northwest Division

	GP	W	L	OT	GF	GA	Pts
Vancouver	82	54	19	9	262	185	117
Calgary	82	41	29	12	250	237	94
Minnesota	82	39	35	8	206	233	86
Colorado	82	30	44	8	227	288	68
Edmonton	82	25	45	12	193	269	62

Pacific Division

	GP	W	L	OT	GF	GA	Pts
San Jose	82	48	25	9	248	213	105
Anaheim	82	47	30	5	239	235	99
Phoenix	82	43	26	13	231	226	99
Los Angeles	82	46	30	6	219	198	98
Dallas	82	42	29	11	227	233	95

October 9	Phoenix 5–Boston 2 (at Prague, Czech Republic)
October 10	Boston 3–Phoenix 0 (at Prague, Czech Republic)
October 16	Boston 4 at New Jersey 1
October 19	Boston 3 at Washington 1
October 21	Washington 1 at Boston 4
October 23	NY Rangers 3 at Boston 2
October 28	Toronto 0 at Boston 2 [Thomas]
October 30	Boston 4 at Ottawa 0 [Thomas]
November 3	Boston 5 at Buffalo 2
November 5	Boston 3 at Washington 5
November 6	St. Louis 2 at Boston 1 (SO)
November 10	Boston 7 at Pittsburgh 4
November 11	Montreal 3 at Boston 1
November 13	Ottawa 2 at Boston 0 [Elliott]
November 15	New Jersey 0 at Boston 3 [Thomas]
November 17	Boston 3 at NY Rangers 2
November 18	Florida 0 at Boston 4 [Rask]
November 20	Los Angeles 4 at Boston 3 (SO)
November 22	Boston 1 at Tampa Bay 3
November 24	Boston 3 at Florida 1
November 26	Carolina 3 at Boston 0 [Ward]
November 28	Boston 1 at Atlanta 4
December 1	Boston 3 at Philadelphia 0 [Thomas]
December 2	Tampa Bay 1 at Boston 8
December 4	Boston 2 at Toronto 3 (SO)
December 7	Buffalo 2 at Boston 3 (Recchi 2:11 OT)
December 9	NY Islanders 2 at Boston 5
December 11	Philadelphia 2 at Boston 1 (Richards 4:57 OT)
December 15	Boston 2 at Buffalo 3
December 16	Boston 3 at Montreal 4
December 18	Washington 2 at Boston 3
December 20	Anaheim 3 at Boston 0 [Hiller]
December 23	Atlanta 1 at Boston 4
December 27	Boston 3 at Florida 2 (SO)
December 28	Boston 4 at Tampa Bay 3
December 30	Boston 2 at Atlanta 3 (SO)
January 1	Boston 6 at Buffalo 7 (SO)
January 3	Boston 2 at Toronto 1
January 6	Minnesota 3 at Boston 1
January 8	Boston 2 at Montreal 3 (Pacioretty 3:43 OT)
January 10	Boston 4 at Pittsburgh 2
January 11	Ottawa 0 at Boston 6 [Thomas]
January 13	Philadelphia 5 at Boston 7
January 15	Pittsburgh 3 at Boston 2
January 17	Carolina 0 at Boston 7 [Thomas]
January 18	Boston 3 at Carolina 2
January 20	Buffalo 4 at Boston 2
January 22	Boston 6 at Colorado 2
January 24	Boston 0 at Los Angeles 2 [Quick]
January 26	Florida 1 at Boston 2
January 30	2011 NHL All-Star Game
February 1	Boston 3 at Carolina 2
February 3	Dallas 3 at Boston 6
February 5	San Jose 2 at Boston 0 [Niemi]
February 9	Montreal 6 at Boston 8
February 11	Detroit 6 at Boston 1
February 13	Boston 2 at Detroit 4
February 15	Toronto 4 at Boston 3
February 17	Boston 6 at NY Islanders 3
February 18	Boston 4 at Ottawa 2
February 22	Boston 3 at Calgary 1
February 26	Boston 3 at Vancouver 1
February 27	Boston 3 at Edmonton 2
March 1	Boston 3 at Ottawa 0 [Rask]
March 3	Tampa Bay 1 at Boston 2
March 5	Pittsburgh 3 at Boston 2 (Jeffrey 1:52 OT)
March 8	Boston 1 at Montreal 4
March 10	Buffalo 4 at Boston 3 (Boyes 3:44 OT)
March 11	Boston 2 at NY Islanders 4
March 15	Boston 3 at Columbus 2 (SO)
March 17	Boston 3 at Nashville 4 (Weber 3:37 OT)
March 19	Boston 2 at Toronto 5
March 22	New Jersey 1 at Boston 4
March 24	Montreal 0 at Boston 7 [Thomas]
March 26	NY Rangers 1 at Boston 0 (Stepan 6:39 1st) [Lundqvist]
March 27	Boston 2 at Philadelphia 1
March 29	Chicago 0 at Boston 3 [Thomas]
March 31	Toronto 4 at Boston 3 (SO)
April 2	Atlanta 2 at Boston 3
April 4	Boston 3 at NY Rangers 5
April 6	NY Islanders 2 at Boston 3
April 9	Ottawa 1 at Boston 3
April 10	Boston 2 at New Jersey 3

	GP	G	A	P	Pim
Milan Lucic	79	30	32	62	121
David Krejci	75	13	49	62	28
Patrice Bergeron	80	22	35	57	26
Nathan Horton	80	26	27	53	85
Mark Recchi	81	14	34	48	35
Zdeno Chara	81	14	30	44	88
Brad Marchand	77	21	20	41	51
Michael Ryder	79	18	23	41	26
Dennis Seidenberg	81	7	25	32	41
Gregory Campbell	80	13	16	29	93
Blake Wheeler	58	11	16	27	32
Tyler Seguin	74	11	11	22	18
Shawn Thornton	79	10	10	20	122
Johnny Boychuk	69	3	13	16	45
Adam McQuaid	67	3	12	15	96
Andrew Ference	70	3	12	15	60

	GP	G	A	P	Pim
Daniel Paille	43	6	7	13	28
Steven Kampfer	38	5	5	10	12
Marc Savard	25	2	8	10	29
Tomas Kaberle	24	1	8	9	2
Rich Peverley	23	4	3	7	2
Jordan Caron	23	3	4	7	6
Chris Kelly	24	2	3	5	6
Mark Stuart	31	1	4	5	23
Matt Hunwick	22	1	2	3	9
Tim Thomas	57	0	3	3	13
Zach Hamill	3	0	1	1	0
Matt Bartkowski	6	0	0	0	4
Tuukka Rask	29	0	0	0	2
Shane Hnidy	3	0	0	0	2
Jamie Arniel	1	0	0	0	0

In Goal

	GP	W-L-OT	Mins	GA	SO	GAA
Tim Thomas	57	35-11-9	3,363:58	112	9	2.00
Tuukka Rask	29	11-14-2	1,594:11	71	2	2.67

Eastern Conference Quarter-Final

(1) Washington vs. (8) NY Rangers

April 13	NY Rangers 1 at Washington 2
	(Semin 18:24 OT)
April 15	NY Rangers 0 at Washington 2 [Neuvirth]
April 17	Washington 2 at NY Rangers 3
April 20	Washington 4 at NY Rangers 3
	(Chimera 32:36 OT)
April 23	NY Rangers 1 at Washington 3

Washington wins best-of-seven 4-1

(2) Philadelphia vs. (7) Buffalo

April 14	Buffalo 1 at Philadelphia 0 [Miller]
April 16	Buffalo 4 at Philadelphia 5
April 18	Philadelphia 4 at Buffalo 2
April 20	Philadelphia 0 at Buffalo 1 [Miller]
April 22	Buffalo 4 at Philadelphia 3 (Ennis 5:31 OT)
April 24	Philadelphia 5 at Buffalo 4 (Leino 4:43 OT)
April 26	Buffalo 2 at Philadelphia 5

Philadelphia wins best-of-seven 4-3

(3) Boston vs. (6) Montreal

April 14	Montreal 2 at Boston 0 [Price]
April 16	Montreal 3 at Boston 1
April 18	Boston 4 at Montreal 2
April 21	Boston 5 at Montreal 4 (Ryder 1:59 OT)
April 23	Montreal 1 at Boston 2 (Horton 29:03 OT)
April 26	Boston 1 at Montreal 2
April 27	Montreal 3 at Boston 4 (Horton 5:43 OT)

Boston wins best-of-seven 4-3

(4) Pittsburgh vs. (5) Tampa Bay

April 13	Tampa Bay 0 at Pittsburgh 3 [Fleury]
April 15	Tampa Bay 5 at Pittsburgh 1
April 18	Pittsburgh 3 at Tampa Bay 2
April 20	Pittsburgh 3 at Tampa Bay 2 (Neal 23:38 OT)
April 23	Tampa Bay 8 at Pittsburgh 2
April 25	Pittsburgh 2 at Tampa Bay 4
April 27	Tampa Bay 1 at Pittsburgh 0 [Roloson]

Tampa Bay wins best-of-seven 4-3

Western Conference Quarter-Final

(1) Vancouver vs. (8) Chicago

April 13	Chicago 0 at Vancouver 2 [Luongo]
April 15	Chicago 3 at Vancouver 4
April 17	Vancouver 3 at Chicago 2
April 19	Vancouver 2 at Chicago 7
April 21	Chicago 5 at Vancouver 0 [Crawford]
April 24	Vancouver 3 at Chicago 4 (B. Smith 15:30 OT)
April 26	Chicago 1 at Vancouver 2 (Burrows 5:22 OT)

Vancouver wins best-of-seven 4-3

(2) San Jose vs. (7) Los Angeles

April 14	Los Angeles 2 at San Jose 3 (Pavelski 14:44 OT)
April 16	Los Angeles 4 at San Jose 0 [Quick]
April 17	San Jose 6 at Los Angeles 5
	(Setoguchi 3:09 OT)
April 21	San Jose 6 at Los Angeles 3
April 23	Los Angeles 3 at San Jose 1
April 25	San Jose 4 at Los Angeles 3
	(Thornton 2:22 OT)

San Jose wins best-of-seven 4-2

(3) Detroit vs. (6) Phoenix

April 13	Phoenix 2 at Detroit 4
April 16	Phoenix 3 at Detroit 4
April 18	Detroit 4 at Phoenix 2
April 20	Detroit 6 at Phoenix 3

Detroit wins best-of-seven 4-0

(4) Anaheim vs. (5) Nashville

April 13	Nashville 4 at Anaheim 1
April 15	Nashville 3 at Anaheim 5
April 17	Anaheim 3 at Nashville 4
April 20	Anaheim 6 at Nashville 3
April 22	Nashville 4 at Anaheim 3 (Smithson 1:57 OT)
April 24	Anaheim 2 at Nashville 4

Nashville wins best-of-seven 4-2

Eastern Conference Semi-Final
(1) Washington vs. (5) Tampa Bay

April 29	Tampa Bay 4 at Washington 2
May 1	Tampa Bay 3 at Washington 2 (Lecavalier 6:19 OT)
May 3	Washington 3 at Tampa Bay 4
May 4	Washington 3 at Tampa Bay 5

Tampa Bay wins best-of-seven 4-0

(2) Philadelphia vs. (3) Boston

April 30	Boston 7 at Philadelphia 3
May 2	Boston 3 at Philadelphia 2 (Krejci 14:00 OT)
May 4	Philadelphia 1 at Boston 5
May 6	Philadelphia 1 at Boston 5

Boston wins best-of-seven 4-0

Eastern Conference Final
(3) Boston vs. (5) Tampa Bay

May 14	Tampa Bay 5 at Boston 2
May 17	Tampa Bay 5 at Boston 6
May 19	Boston 2 at Tampa Bay 0 [Thomas]
May 21	Boston 3 at Tampa Bay 5
May 23	Tampa Bay 1 at Boston 3
May 25	Boston 4 at Tampa Bay 5
May 27	Tampa Bay 0 at Boston 1

Boston wins best-of-seven 4-3

Western Conference Semi-Final
(1) Vancouver vs. (5) Nashville

April 28	Nashville 0 at Vancouver 1 [Luongo]
April 30	Nashville 2 at Vancouver 1 (Halischuk 34:51 OT)
May 3	Vancouver 3 at Nashville 2 (Kesler 10:45 OT)
May 5	Vancouver 4 at Nashville 2
May 7	Nashville 4 at Vancouver 3
May 9	Vancouver 2 at Nashville 1

Vancouver wins best-of-seven 4-2

(2) San Jose vs. (3) Detroit

April 29	Detroit 1 at San Jose 2 (Ferriero 7:03 OT)
May 1	Detroit 1 at San Jose 2
May 4	San Jose 4 at Detroit 3 (Setoguchi 9:21 OT)
May 6	San Jose 3 at Detroit 4
May 8	Detroit 4 at San Jose 3
May 10	San Jose 1 at Detroit 3
May 12	Detroit 2 at San Jose 3

San Jose wins best-of-seven 4-3

Western Conference Final
(1) Vancouver vs. (2) San Jose

May 15	San Jose 2 at Vancouver 3
May 18	San Jose 3 at Vancouver 7
May 20	Vancouver 3 at San Jose 4
May 22	Vancouver 4 at San Jose 2
May 24	San Jose 2 at Vancouver 3 (Bieksa 30:18 OT)

Vancouver wins best-of-seven 4-1

Stanley Cup Final
(1) Vancouver vs. (3) Boston

June 1	Boston 0 at Vancouver 1 [Luongo]
June 4	Boston 2 at Vancouver 3 (Burrows 0:11 OT)
June 6	Vancouver 1 at Boston 8
June 8	Vancouver 0 at Boston 4 [Thomas]
June 10	Boston 0 at Vancouver 1 [Luongo]
June 13	Vancouver 2 at Boston 5
June 15	Boston 4 at Vancouver 0 [Thomas]

Boston wins best-of-seven 4-3

FINAL STATISTICS, PLAYOFFS

	GP	G	A	P	Pim
David Krejci	25	12	11	23	10
Patrice Bergeron	23	6	14	20	28
Brad Marchand	25	11	8	19	40
Nathan Horton	21	8	9	17	35
Michael Ryder	25	8	9	17	8
Mark Recchi	25	5	9	14	8
Chris Kelly	25	5	8	13	6
Milan Lucic	25	5	7	12	63
Rich Peverley	25	4	8	12	17
Dennis Seidenberg	25	1	10	11	31
Tomas Kaberle	25	0	11	11	4

	GP	G	A	P	Pim
Andrew Ference	25	4	6	10	37
Johnny Boychuk	25	3	6	9	12
Zdeno Chara	24	2	7	9	34
Tyler Seguin	13	3	4	7	2
Daniel Paille	25	3	3	6	4
Gregory Campbell	25	1	3	4	4
Adam McQuaid	23	0	4	4	14
Shawn Thornton	18	0	1	1	24
Shane Hnidy	3	0	0	0	7
Tim Thomas	25	0	0	0	4

In Goal

	GP	W-L-OT	Mins	GA	SO	GAA
Tim Thomas	25	16-9	1,541:53	51	4	1.98

By Draft

Jamie Arniel
Selected 97th overall at 2008 Entry Draft

Patrice Bergeron
Selected 45th overall at 2003 Entry Draft

Jordan Caron
Selected 25th overall at 2009 Entry Draft

Zach Hamill
Selected 8th overall at 2007 Entry Draft

Matt Hunwick
Selected 224th overall at 2004 Entry Draft

David Krejci
Selected 63rd overall at 2004 Entry Draft

Milan Lucic
Selected 50th overall at 2006 Entry Draft

Brad Marchand
Selected 71st overall at 2006 Entry Draft

Tyler Seguin
Selected 2nd overall at 2010 Entry Draft

By Free Agent Signing

Zdeno Chara
Signed as a free agent on July 1, 2006

Shane Hnidy
Signed as a free agent on February 26, 2011

Michael Ryder
Signed as a free agent on July 1, 2008

Marc Savard
Signed as a free agent on July 1, 2006

Tim Thomas
Signed as a free agent on September 14, 2005

Shawn Thornton
Signed as a free agent on July 1, 2007

Blake Wheeler
Signed as a free agent on July 1, 2008

By Trade

Matt Bartkowski
Acquired from Florida on March 3, 2010, with Dennis Seidenberg for Craig Weller, Byron Bitz, and a 2nd-round draft choice in 2010

Johnny Boychuk
Acquired from Colorado on June 24, 2008, for Matt Hendricks

Gregory Campbell
Acquired from Florida on June 22, 2010, with Nathan Horton for Dennis Wideman, a 1st-round draft choice in 2010, and a 3rd-round draft choice in 2011

Andrew Ference
Acquired from Calgary on February 10, 2007, with Chuck Kobasew for Brad Stuart, Wayne Primeau, and a 4th-round draft choice in 2008

Nathan Horton
Acquired from Florida on June 22, 2010, with Gregory Campbell for Dennis Wideman, a 1st-round draft choice in 2010, and a 3rd-round draft choice in 2011

Tomas Kaberle
Acquired from Toronto on February 18, 2011, for Joe Colborne, a 1st-round draft choice in 2011, and a conditional 2nd-round draft choice

Steven Kampfer
Acquired from Anaheim on March 2, 2010, for a 4th-round draft choice in 2010

Chris Kelly
Acquired from Ottawa on February 15, 2011, for a 2nd-round draft choice in 2011

Adam McQuaid
Acquired from Columbus on May 16, 2007, for a 5th-round draft choice in 2007

Daniel Paille
Acquired from Buffalo on October 20, 2009, for a 3rd-round draft choice in 2010

Rich Peverley
Acquired from Atlanta on February 18, 2011, with Boris Valabik for Blake Wheeler and Mark Stuart

Tuukka Rask
Acquired from Toronto on June 24, 2006, for Andrew Raycroft

Mark Recchi
Acquired from Tampa Bay on March 4, 2009, with a 2nd-round draft choice in 2010 for Matt Lashoff and Martins Karsums

Dennis Seidenberg
Acquired from Florida on March 3, 2010, with Matt Bartkowski for Craig Weller, Byron Bitz, and a 2nd-round draft choice in 2010

	GP	G	A	P	Pim
Jamie Arniel	78	23	27	50	26
Zach Hamill	68	9	34	43	66
Maxime Sauve	61	21	17	38	36
Kirk MacDonald	76	15	23	38	48
Trent Whitfield	45	18	18	36	42
Jordan Caron	47	12	16	28	16
Jordan LaVallee-Smotherman	71	14	12	26	68
Joe Colborne	55	12	14	26	35
Jeremy Reich	72	14	9	23	52
David Ling	56	8	15	23	55
Matt Bartkowski	69	5	18	23	42
Lane MacDermid	78	7	12	19	158
Yuri Alexandrov	66	6	13	19	44
Jeff Penner	57	5	14	19	30
Steven Kampfer	22	3	13	16	12
Andrew Bodnarchuk	75	1	15	16	91
Jordan Knackstedt	22	7	5	12	12
Colby Cohen	46	1	11	12	46
Wyatt Smith	30	2	7	9	23
Alain Goulet	16	2	6	8	10
Antoine Roussel	42	1	7	8	88
Levi Nelson	14	4	3	7	19
Stefan Chaput	15	3	4	7	4
David Laliberte	17	1	5	6	14

	GP	G	A	P	Pim
Brian McGrattan	39	4	1	5	97
Sean Zimmerman	23	0	4	4	23
Ryan Spooner	3	2	1	3	0
Kyle MacKinnon	5	1	2	3	2
Nathan McIver	60	0	3	3	176
Jeff LoVecchio	22	0	3	3	9
David Warsofsky	10	0	3	3	6
Carter Camper	3	1	1	2	2
Boris Valabik	10	0	2	2	24
Ryan Donald	13	0	2	2	13
Adam Estoclet	7	0	2	2	7
Jared Knight	3	0	2	2	2
Nolan Schaefer	30	0	1	1	6
Ryan Button	7	0	1	1	2
Cody Wild	7	0	1	1	2
Matt Dalton	16	0	1	1	0
Kevan Miller	6	0	0	0	9
Juraj Simek	11	0	0	0	6
Anton Khudobin	16	0	0	0	2
Yannick Riendeau	6	0	0	0	2
Maury Edwards	3	0	0	0	2
Michael Hutchinson	28	0	0	0	0
Devin Timberlake	2	0	0	0	0

In Goal

	GP	W-L-OT	Mins	GA	SO	GAA
Tanton Khudobin	16	9-4-1	901	36	1	2.40
Nolan Schaefer	30	9-16-1	1,604	83	0	3.11
Michael Hutchinson	28	13-10-1	1,476	77	1	3.13
Matt Dalton	16	7-9-0	862	46	2	3.20

STANLEY CUP PLAYOFFS 2011 NHL

GAME ONE — *April 14, 2011*

Montreal 2 at Boston 0
(Montreal leads series 1–0)

One of the oldest and most contested rivalries in sport, Boston and Montreal went at it again in a best-of-seven series, and this time the visiting Habs drew first blood. During the regular season there was little difference between the teams. Boston finished first place in the Northeast Division with 46 wins and 103 points, while Montreal was second with 44 wins and 96 points. Both teams had the success they had thanks in large measure to their goalies, and that proved the difference tonight.

It wasn't so much that Tim Thomas had a bad night for Boston as that Carey Price was excellent for the Canadiens. Price also had the benefit of some more intense play from his teammates inside their own blue-line, as just about every skater on Montreal recorded at least one blocked shot. The final tally was nineteen blocked shots for the Habs, far more than Boston, who had yet to get into playoff mode.

Boston's Patrice Bergeron collides with Lars Eller as both players fight for position.

Conference Quarter-Final — Boston Bruins vs. Montreal Canadiens

21

"It's playoff time, and that is what it is all about," Montreal's Brent Sopel suggested. "It's battling for one another and it's sacrifice. I've always said, blocking shots hurts, but if it hits me, it's not going in the net. That's what you have to do. It's all about playing solid and sacrificing yourself."

As well, Montreal managed to get that vital first goal, which came thanks to Brian Gionta, just 2:44 into the game. And it came off a play that highlighted the difference in intensity between the two teams this game. The Canadiens made a simple dump-in of the puck into the Boston end, but defenceman Tomas Kaberle was too casual in retrieving it and was outmuscled by Scott Gomez. He fired the puck to the front of the net where Brian Gionta had plenty of time to beat Thomas.

Action heats up around Montreal goalie Carey Price as Rich Peverley of Boston (#49) competes with Jaroslav Spacek for the puck.

Boston goalie Tim Thomas watches the puck go wide and looks for the play to come back into his crease area.

The Gomez to Gionta combination worked again late in the third period to give the Habs the only goals they'd need. This time it was a Milan Lucic giveaway just inside the Bruins blue-line, and Gionta's shot, from farther out, might have been stopped by Thomas on another night.

As it was, Price settled in and stopped all thirty-one shots, and the Canadiens played stifling defence in front of him. "He had a lot of great saves for them out there," said Boston's Brad Marchand. "He was a difference-maker for them. He's a great goalie, one of the best in the league."

Forward Patrice Bergeron put his finger on the Bruins' troubles. "I thought our chances were good," he offered. "I thought our shots were good, but we didn't have enough traffic. So I don't think our shots were too much from the outside. We had some chances from the slot; it's just he [Price] could see the puck."

Conference Quarter-Final — Boston Bruins vs. Montreal Canadiens

23

GAME TWO — *April 16, 2011*

Montreal 3 at Boston 1

(Montreal leads series 2–0)

Normally, when the home team loses the first two games in a best-of-seven series, the news is nothing short of shocking. But when Montreal does the trick to Boston, it's more de rigeur than anything else. Montreal had won twenty-four of thirty-two playoff series since the Bruins joined the NHL in 1924, and this seemed to be just another in a long line of victories. With the 2–0 lead, Montreal now headed home for a chance to eliminate the Bruins on home ice.

"We are just keeping our game really simple and we are just getting pucks to the net on Timmy [Thomas] and we are getting guys there, and we have been getting the bounces so far this series and we are getting lucky," said Montreal goalie Carey Price. "We are playing really well defensively, and we just have to keep doing what we are doing."

For the Bruins, the team was jolted by the pre-game news that captain and giant defenceman Zdeno Chara was too dehydrated to play. His spot was taken by Shane Hnidy, a late-season addition to the team, but he played only a few shifts as coach Claude Julien went with five defencemen most of the night.

The impact of playing without Chara was felt right away as Montreal jumped into a 1–0 lead just forty-three seconds after the opening faceoff. It came on a clever, heads-up play from James Wisneiwski. He fired a long shot on goal, but kept it low to create a rebound for Mike Cammalleri, who was unchecked and heading

Carey Price loses control of the puck and falls while David Krejci scoops the loose puck in behind the Montreal net.

24

Conference Quarter-Final — Boston Bruins vs. Montreal Canadiens

Brian Gionta (left) and Johnny Boychuk go into the boards for the puck in a photograph captured through a camera opening in the glass.

Conference Quarter-Final — Boston Bruins vs. Montreal Canadiens

25

towards the goal on the other side. Indeed, Thomas kicked the rebound out, and Cammalleri converted quickly before the goalie could cover the open side.

Less than two minutes later, Mathieu Darche made it 2–0 on a nice pass from Cammalleri while Dennis Seidenberg was in the penalty box for interference. Again, with the early lead, the Habs were able to dictate play, protecting goalie Carey Price and making it nearly impossible for the Bruins to penetrate the front of the Montreal net.

The Bruins finally got on the scoreboard early in the second period when Patrice Bergeron got his stick on the ice and Brad Marchand fired a hard pass that looked like a shot. Bergeron made the perfect re-direct to get the score close, but a goal by Yannick Weber late in the second restored the Canadiens two-goal lead.

P.K. Subban had the only penalty of the third period but the Bruins couldn't convert. Price was the busier of the goalies, he stopped thirty-four of thirty-five shots and was again better than his counterpart Thomas. To make matters worse, Boston was 0–26 in series in which it trailed 2–0. The future was not looking bright for the Bruins at all.

"If we're sitting here happy about [being up 2–0] and celebrating, then we are making a crucial mistake," said Cammalleri. "You can be happy, and the fans can be happy, and our parents and family can be happy, and good for them. But we have no time to be happy right now."

Boston's Brad Marchand carries the puck down the left wing while looking for a play in front of the Montreal goal.

GAME THREE — *April 18, 2011*

Boston 4 at Montreal 2

(Montreal leads series 2–1)

For the third time in the series, it was the road team that scored an early goal to take the home crowd out of the game and set the pace the rest of the way. For Boston, it couldn't have come at a better time. To have fallen behind 3–0 would have more or less handed the series win to the Canadiens, but now the Bruins were still very much alive and in contention.

As in the first two games, the difference was goaltending as Carey Price had a weak outing while Tim Thomas was sensational. The first goal came on a great pass from Patrice Bergeron to David Krejci at 3:11, and then midway through the period Nathan Horton banked a shot off Price and in, a shot the goalie should save 99 times out of 100. The three players involved in these goals represented the Bruins' number-one line, and after two very quiet games, they showed up to play in a big way when it counted the most.

"You have to realize there are some challenges in the playoffs with a lot tighter checking and a lot tighter matchups," said Boston coach Claude Julien. "Then you've got a guy like Nathan Horton who's in his first playoffs, so this was his third playoff game, and what I saw is a guy getting better. After he scored that goal, it certainly took a lot of weight off his shoulders. Hopefully they can build on that."

Boston goalie Tim Thomas has to be at his best to keep sight of the puck while dealing with heavy traffic in his crease.

Conference Quarter-Final — Boston Bruins vs. Montreal Canadiens

27

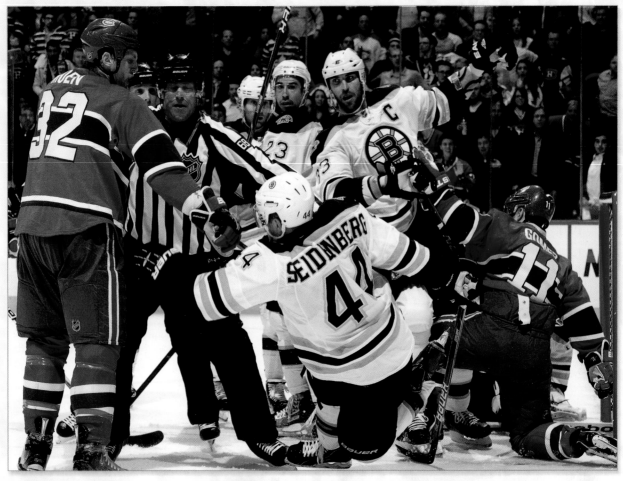

Emotions run high as players from both sides push and shove after a whistle during a critical moment in game three.

To make matters worse, Price made a bad giveaway early in the third and Rich Peverley controlled the puck and whipped it into the empty net for a 3–0 lead. It was a goal uncharacteristic of Price, who had an outstanding season, but it was exactly the kind of break the Bruins lacked in the first two games.

"We didn't compete in the first thirty minutes," Montreal coach Jacques Martin conceded. "I told the players this morning it was a good thing we weren't playing this morning, because we weren't ready."

And on the topic of big, captain Zdeno Chara was back in the lineup after getting his virus and dehydration under control. "You can ask any player that plays against him," proposed Julien. "He's not an easy guy to play against."

Once they were up 3–0, though, the Bruins learned the hard way that sitting on a lead is not the best playoff strategy. Andrei Kostitsyn got one goal back later in the second period, and then Tomas Plekanec beat Thomas from a bad angle to give the Habs life. It was a terrible goal for Thomas to give up, but he made amends by making several great saves down the stretch as the Bruins held on for the win. Cases in point were critical stops late in the game on Andrei Kostitsyn and Scott Gomez.

"He made some big saves," Julien said of his goalie's late-game heroics. "The fact he was able to do that shows a lot of character because there's no doubt he'd like to have those two goals back. A goaltender could have just had negative thoughts in his mind and not been sharp in the end. For him to do what he did showed he was willing to redeem himself."

Chris Kelly scored an empty netter with 25.6 seconds left in the game, and the Bruins were back in it despite a letdown in the second half of the game.

Rich Peverley celebrates a goal during Boston's crucial win in game three.

Conference Quarter-Final — Boston Bruins vs. Montreal Canadiens

29

GAME FOUR — *April 21, 2011*

Boston 5 at Montreal 4
(series tied 2–2)

In what turned out to be a pivotal game in the series—and the most entertaining—the Boston Bruins overcame three Montreal leads in the game and won in overtime thanks to Michael Ryder's second goal of the game. Ryder, a former Canadiens forward, enjoyed the role of spoiler more than a little bit at the Bell Centre, and the Bruins won back-to-back games despite losing all three games in the regular season in Montreal.

Indeed, it was Boston's third line of Ryder–Chris Kelly–Rich Peverley that caused most of the damage

tonight. In addition to Ryder's two goals (and an assist), Kelly had a goal and two assists, and Peverley contributed two assists.

"That whole line was really good for us tonight," agreed coach Claude Julien.

Brent Sopel got the only goal of the first period, the first time in the series that the home side escaped the opening twenty minutes with a lead. The goal came on a long, hard shot in a period dominated by the Habs, but the second period was far crazier and more undisciplined, much to the delight of fans not necessarily emotionally attached to one team.

Ryder got his first of the game and series at 2:13 off a wrist shot that tied the game, but the Canadiens pulled ahead with two quick goals from Mike

Montreal's David Desharnais loses his balance as he tries to make a play near the Boston net.

30

Conference Quarter-Final — Boston Bruins vs. Montreal Canadiens

Goalie Tim Thomas watches the play as his defenceman Andrew Ference reaches to clear the puck out of harm's way.

Conference Quarter-Final — Boston Bruins vs. Montreal Canadiens

31

Patrice Bergeron (left) and Brad Marchand celebrate a goal during Boston's win in game four to even the series.

Cammalleri and Andrei Kostitsyn less than a minute apart. By this time, the Habs had a 29–12 shots on goal advantage and were clearly the better team.

The Bruins, though, realized what was at stake, and if they were to have any chance to win this series, now was the time they had to step up. Coach Claude Julien called a timeout to remind his charges of what was going on, and they responded appropriately. Andrew Ference got one goal back two minutes after Kostitsyn's score with a shot from the blue-line that eluded Carey Price, and then Patrice Bergeron tied the game at 17:04. That set the stage for a crazy third period.

"We had to find a way to have huge shift to get the momentum back, and we did that," Bergeron noted. "Then, we went from there and got the big goal," he added, referring to Ference's vital score.

Key to the comeback was a sense by the Bruins that Montreal had felt victory was in hand with the score

3–1. But the Habs knew from their own experience, from game three when they nearly overcame a 3–0 deficit, that the game isn't over until the final horn. Still, if they dominated the first half of the game, they allowed the Bruins to control the second half and overtime.

For a third time Montreal took the lead, this time courtesy of a P.K. Subban goal on the power play at 1:39. Undaunted, Boston again tied the game thanks to Kelly, who had to wear a full shield to protect a tender face after sliding awkwardly into the post the previous game.

That set the stage for Ryder's winner just 1:59 into overtime as his quick shot beat Price cleanly. A series that looked so clearly to be in Montreal's favour was now tied, and the Bruins had re-claimed home-ice advantage for the final three games. Boston was going home—and it had the momentum as well.

GAME FIVE — April 23, 2011

Montreal 1 at **Boston 2**

(Boston leads series 3–2)

In a 2–2 series, game five is always the most important because the winner then is in a position to win the next game to close out the series. Things were no different this night, and because of the game's importance, both teams produced their best game. The result was a double overtime classic that had great plays, great goaltending, and a dramatic finish.

Nathan Horton was the hero, scoring the winning goal at 9:03 of the fifth period to give the Bruins their third win in a row and their second straight win in overtime. But it was a game dominated by the goalies—and decided by their mistakes or lack thereof.

The game was without a goal for the first two periods thanks to Tim Thomas at the Boston end and Carey Price at the Montreal end. Both kept the game scoreless with key saves, and in Thomas's case he got some help in the first period from Michael Ryder. With Thomas out of his crease, Ryder got his hand in front of a shot that was going into the empty net, keeping the game 0–0.

It was the home Bruins who struck first, early in the third period. Brad Marchand collected a rebound and snapped the puck in at 4:33, and it seemed that might be all the Bruins needed. Boston stepped up and played solid defence the rest of the way, but

Down but not out, Tim Thomas keeps his eye on the puck after making a save.

Conference Quarter-Final — Boston Bruins vs. Montreal Canadiens

33

Montreal's Scott Gomez lunges across his crease to prevent Rich Peverley from getting a shot on Carey Price.

Montreal didn't give up, either. Jeff Halpern finally tied the game at 13:56 when his low shot eluded Thomas, and that was all the scoring through regulation time. Teams played cautiously in the first overtime, but in the second, play opened up.

Thomas made the save of the series early in the fifth period when he got his left pad out on a Brian Gionta shot. It was a one-timer on a two-on-one and looked to be the game winner as soon as the puck left Gionta's stick—but Thomas had other ideas.

"As soon as it left my stick, I thought it was going in," Gionta admitted. The opposite perspective was equally honest. "If it's not for Tim Thomas, we're not standing here right now," said Boston defenceman Dennis Seidenberg.

Less than four minutes later, Andrew Ference took a pass from Milan Lucic just inside the Montreal blue-line as he was being checked. Ference let go a long shot that Price kicked out, giving Nathan Horton a generous rebound. He buried the shot, and the game was over. The Bruins had a 3–2 series lead.

"I saw the rebound come out," Horton described. "It was like it's in slow motion. It was just sitting there. I'll tell you, it felt good to put that in the net. Obviously winning the game, it was a pretty special moment."

Shots on goal favoured Boston 51–45, but of those 96 total shots, only three found the back of the net. That was great goaltending, and Thomas was just one save better on this night.

"You can say it is too bad because we played well and we didn't win," opined Mathieu Darche of Montreal, "but, then again, we know we had all those chances. Law of average, at one point, one will go in. And Timmy Thomas made some great saves. Carey made some great saves. It was the lower-scoring game of the series, but it is probably the game with the most chances, both sides."

Brad Marchand whoops it up after taking Boston to a 1-0 lead early in the third period.

GAME SIX — *April 26, 2011*

Boston 1 at **Montreal 2**

(series tied 3–3)

For the first time in the series, it was special teams and not goaltending that decided a game, and on this night the Habs had all the luck and the Bruins none. In the end, Montreal scored two goals in five-on-three situations and Boston went 0-for-4 with the man advantage, and that was the difference in the game, plain and simple.

"They scored two goals five-on-three," Boston coach Claude Julien summarized. "Five-on-four, they weren't a threat and neither were we. Five-on-five, I thought we were obviously a team that held most of the control in the game, and that's what we have to do. We have to stay disciplined, stay away from the penalty box like we talked about at the beginning of the series."

Discipline was definitely a missing element from the Boston execution of its game plan tonight. In the first period, Adam McQuaid caused a too-many-men penalty, and just four seconds later Dennis Seidenberg took a slashing penalty. The Habs connected a minute into the lengthy two-man advantage when Mike Cammalleri was perfectly set up for a one-timer by

Michael Ryder unleashes a shot against Montreal in game six.

36

Conference Quarter-Final — Boston Bruins vs. Montreal Canadiens

Mike Cammalleri wins a faceoff from Patrice Bergeron in the Montreal end.

Conference Quarter-Final — Boston Bruins vs. Montreal Canadiens

37

P.K. Subban, blowing a shot past Tim Thomas from the top of the right circle.

Dennis Seidenberg tied the game for Boston in the first minute of the second period when he caught Carey Price napping on a wraparound, but soon after the Bruins lost their momentum when they ran into more penalty trouble. This was more serious. Milan Lucic drove Jaroslav Spacek into the glass from behind and was assessed a five-minute major for boarding and a game misconduct. Then, just sixteen seconds later, Patrice Bergeron fired the puck over the glass to earn a delay-of-game penalty, and with a two-minute two-man advantage the Habs struck again.

On this occasion it was Brian Gionta who got to a rebound after Thomas had made a fine save but couldn't control the puck. The Habs then took the next three minors in the period but Boston was unable to mount a serious power play. The goalless game with the man advantage meant the team was now 0-for-19 in the series.

In the third period, the Habs played solid defence, stayed out of the penalty box, and had a big period from Price, who closed the door on all shots and took his team to victory, forcing a seventh game back in Boston.

Said Julien: "It's one of those games where we tried, we worked hard, we had our chances and we weren't able to bury them. But we're certainly not down or disappointed in our game, except for the fact those five-on-threes ended up costing us the game."

Dennis Seidenberg tries to come out in front and stuff the puck in, but goalie Carey Price is ready to make the save.

GAME SEVEN — *April 27, 2011*

Montreal 3 at **Boston 4**

*(**Boston** wins series 4–3)*

The decisive game in the series somehow mirrored the series itself. That is, Montreal held a 2–0 lead in games only to see Boston tie it, but the Bruins went ahead 3–2 only to see the Canadiens tie it. Tonight's decisive game saw Boston run out to a 2–0 lead and have the Habs tie it, and then gain a 3–2 lead, which they couldn't hold either. In the end, Nathan Horton got his second overtime goal of the series and Boston won all three overtime games played, and the Bruins moved on to face Philadelphia while the Habs were sent to the golf course.

"I think we showed a lot of character," Boston forward Patrice Bergeron noted. "Like I said, we had to put ourselves in a little bubble, and don't think about the pressure and what people were saying around us. I think we did a great job with that. We stayed resilient all game and all series and found a way."

Indeed, they did, but it wasn't easy. The Bruins used the roaring crowd to jump into an early 2–0 lead thanks to goals from Johnny Boychuk at 3:31 and Mark Recchi at 5:33. But the Habs converted a power play with Michael Ryder in the penalty box for hooking, and Yannick Weber beat Tim Thomas with a quick shot to make it 2–1.

The Habs got the only goal of the middle period, a short-handed marker at that, thanks to Tomas

Mark Recchi celebrates a goal while Scott Gomez kneels helplessly in front of his goal.

The Bruins celebrate their game seven victory which took them into the next round of the playoffs and eliminated the Habs.

Plekanec. Chris Kelly looked like he was going to be the hero when he scored midway through the final period on a nice backhander, giving Boston a 3–2 lead with a little more than ten minutes left in regulation.

Bergeron, however, took a high-sticking penalty at 17:23 and defenceman P.K. Subban launched a rocket shot from the point that beat Thomas with just 1:57 left, setting the stage for an overtime which seemed to favour Montreal, based on the team's ability to overcome Boston leads of 2–0 and 3–2.

"We did have the momentum," Subban agreed. "It was pretty clear. We were chipping pucks in and we were getting opportunities, but you know, like I said, just opportunities at this point. You hate to look back at the game and talk about certain situations in the game. Obviously we had opportunities to win it and so did they, and in the end they capitalized. "

Less than six minutes into the fourth period, Horton's long shot found its way through traffic and beat a screened Carey Price. "It felt pretty good," Horton exuded. "I don't remember too much. I remember Milan [Lucic] coming up with the puck, and I just tried to get open. I tried putting the puck towards the net. Luckily it got deflected off someone and it went straight in. That's all I remember. It was pretty special. It doesn't get any better."

The win set up a rematch of the previous year against Philadelphia, a series the Bruins had jumped to a 3–0 lead in, only to lose in seven games. One thing seemed certain—Boston had to get its power play working. It went 0-for-21 against Montreal and became the first team in NHL history to win a seven-game series without scoring so much as a single extra-man goal.

Montreal's Carey Price congratulates his opponent, Tim Thomas, after game seven.

Conference Quarter-Final — Boston Bruins vs. Montreal Canadiens

GAME ONE — *April 30, 2011*

Boston 7 at Philadelphia 3

(Boston leads series 1–0)

It was only a year ago that a great start to the Boston–Philadelphia series for the Bruins quickly turned into a nightmare. The Bruins won the first three games, but in the third of those lost David Krejci with a dislocated wrist thanks to a hard check from Mike Richards. Philly then proceeded to win the next four games and, with the historic comeback, eliminate a stunned Boston team.

"I try not to think about what happened last year but it's in the back of my head," Krejci admitted. "You don't forget these things that often, but I try not to think about it almost at all. It's hard but I just try to stay focused for the game, and my teammates helped me out today."

This year the Bruins vowed things would be different, and they proved as much in game one, scoring early and never letting up en route to an emphatic 7–3 win. And that same Krejci led the attack with two goals and two assists. Linemates Nathan Horton, with a goal and assist, and Brad Marchand, two goals, were also key to the victory.

Boston's Brad Marchand is stopped by Flyers' goalie Brian Boucher.

42

Conference Semi-Final — Boston Bruins vs. Philadelphia Flyers

Two captains meet, Philadelphia's Mike Richards and Zdeno Chara.

Krejci got the first goal at 1:52, when he took Horton's pass and roofed a backhander over Brian Boucher. Midway through the period, Daniel Briere tied the game while the teams were playing four-on-four, but the Bruins regained the advantage with only 35.7 seconds left in the period thanks to Horton. The play started with Dennis Seidenberg in control of the puck behind Boucher's goal. Seidenberg made a nice pass to Krejci in the slot, but Boucher made the save. The puck bounced off his arm, though, and Horton smacked it in out of mid-air.

The Bruins poured it on in the second, scoring early to make it 3–1 and adding two late goals to make it 5–1. Mark Recchi gave the Bruins a two-goal lead when his low shot beat Boucher, and Krejci made it 4–1 by winning the faceoff back to Adam McQuaid at the point and then tipping McQuaid's point shot in. Another point shot and deflection gave Marchand an empty net for a 5–1 lead, after which Flyers' coach Peter Laviolette pulled Boucher in favour of Sergei Bobrovsky.

The Flyers responded with a quick goal just a few seconds later and made it a 5–3 game early in the third, but there would be no miracle comeback this night. Marchand and Gregory Campbell scored later in the third to put an exclamation mark on a huge victory.

Conference Semi-Final — Boston Bruins vs. Philadelphia Flyers

43

Krejci had just a single goal in the seven-game series against Montreal but his rejuvenated play this night was the key for the Bruins. "I think he's more of a quiet person," coach Claude Julien described. "But, you know, once you've had him for a long time, you know his demeanor, you know how he operates. He's a very quiet kid, but he's a very determined individual. There's times where he puts so much pressure on himself that it doesn't always help him. But once he finds his stride,

he's a very determined player. Hopefully this game this afternoon has really helped him."

Flyers coach Peter Laviolette refused to panic, though. He believed there was still plenty of hockey left in the series. "It wasn't a good afternoon all around for all of us," he admitted. "We didn't get any breaks, and we certainly didn't play all that well. At the same time, I don't see the need for a change. We'll see what happens."

The Bruins celebrate their surprisingly easy 7-3 win over the Flyers to take early control of the series.

GAME TWO — *May 2, 2011*

Boston 3 at Philadelphia 2

(Boston leads series 2–0)

David Krejci looked like he had something to prove against the Flyers. For the second straight game, he was the difference, and tonight that difference came in the form of an overtime goal to give Boston a 3–2 win in the game and a huge 2–0 win in the series thanks to two road games.

Krejci converted a pass from Nathan Horton with a wicked shot that beat Brian Boucher high. The puck went in and out so quickly the referee called no goal. The play was reviewed at the next stoppage and video review showed the puck had gone in at 14:00 of the first overtime. The Flyers now had to travel to Boston down two games.

"I wanted to get a good one-timer and it worked," Krejci said. "I thought it was in, but then they kept playing, so I just wanted to finish up on the shift and then the ref took a look at it and it was in."

It was a game the Flyers really should have won. After playing "God Bless America" instead of the national anthem, the Flyers stormed to a lead twenty-nine seconds after the opening faceoff thanks to James van Riemsdyk. The play started at the Philadelphia blue-line when Nikolai Zherdev chipped the puck into centre ice, creating a two-on-one for Claude Giroux and van Riemsdyk, with the only Boston player back being forward Patrice Bergeron. Giroux waited for the perfect moment and slid a pass across that his teammate had only to redirect into the back side of the net.

Midway through the period van Riemsdyk made it 2–0 on a power play. Goalie Tim Thomas couldn't find a point shot, and in the scramble that ensued, van Riemsdyk got a shot off that found the back of the net.

Incredibly, though, the Bruins found a way to get back in the game. Just three and a half minutes after van Riemsdyk's second goal, Chris Kelly knocked in a loose puck when Brian Boucher couldn't control Tomas Kaberle's point shot. Just eighty-five seconds

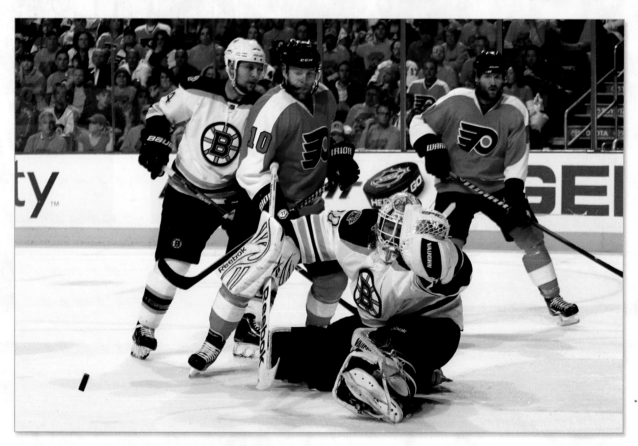

Tim Thomas, outside his blue ice, cuts down the angle to make a good pad save.

Conference Semi-Final — Boston Bruins vs. Philadelphia Flyers

45

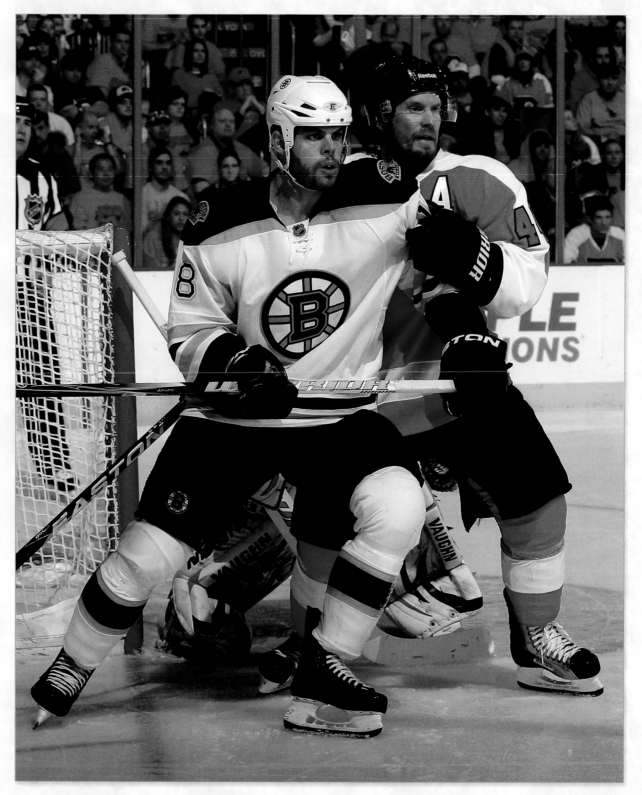

Boston's Nathan Horton and Kimmo Timonen completely obscure the sightlines for goalie Brian Boucher.

Zdeno Chara and Andrej Meszaros fight for the puck behind the Boston goal.

later, the mini-comeback was complete. Bergeron fed Brad Marchand a pass, and his shot from the faceoff circle snuck by Boucher.

"We knew they would have a big start," Marchand conceded. "We knew they were going to come out hard in the first period. We just wanted to weather the storm. It was great we were able to tie it up there. It was pretty bad there at one point. We did a great job of coming back and settled things down and got into the game."

The rest of the game might well have been sub-titled The Tim Thomas Show. He was the one and only reason the Flyers didn't win by several goals in regulation. In the third period alone the Flyers outshot Boston 22–7, but time and again, Thomas was there to make a huge save. The Bruins got the only two penalties of the third period, one early and one to Zdeno Chara with just 2:39 left, but Thomas was

sensational and forced the overtime with his play. In all, he stopped fifty-two of fifty-four shots fired his way.

"He was by far the star of the game," agreed Boston coach Claude Julien. "He made some outstanding saves, especially when they started coming at us. They had some unbelievable scoring chances, he stood tall and he made some great saves. And no doubt, if it's not for Timmy we might not be standing here tonight with a win. But that's what goaltenders do for you in the playoffs and that's what you like to see in order to certainly develop some confidence for your team. We know that the goaltender is there to bail you out and it certainly builds a lot of confidence and Tim has given us that."

As a result, Krejci was able to get the game winner in OT, but make no mistake—this was a goalie's victory as well.

Conference Semi-Final — Boston Bruins vs. Philadelphia Flyers

47

GAME THREE — *May 4, 2011*

Philadelphia 1 at **Boston 5**

(Boston leads series 3–0)

There is always a psychological element that comes into play prior to every playoff game. Game one is so important because you want to get a good start. The second game is important to take control of the series. But really, when a team is ahead 2–0, the third game is absolutely critical to the trailing team because rallying from 3–0 down has happened only three times in seventy years.

Helping the Boston cause was the absence of towering defenceman Chris Pronger, who remained sidelined with an injury. He was the straw that stirred the Philly drink, and without him the Flyers' end was an easier place to skate, no doubt.

Yet the Flyers were one of those teams to pull off such an unlikely comeback, last year against Boston, to boot. The chances of doing it again? Slimmer than none. The Bruins realized this, and they got off to the perfect start, scoring twice in the first sixty-three seconds and roaring away with a 5–1 win that put them in full control of the series.

Captain Zdeno Chara started the night off with a slapshot from the top of the circle just thirty seconds into the game. If the Flyers' goalie had any sense, he'd have closed his eyes or stepped out of the way of the hardest shot in hockey. When the tallest and strongest player in the league has time to wind up for a full slapshot, thirty feet away, only luck and a prayer can help a goalie make the save. And this time, Boucher wasn't so fortunate. Boston 1, Philadelphia 0.

Just thirty-three seconds later, David Krejci got his fourth goal of the series to put the Bruins in charge, and they played incredible defence as well. Boston doubled its lead late in the second period thanks to goals from Daniel Paille and Nathan Horton just a minute and a half apart. That was the end for Boucher as Sergei Bobrovsky came on for the third time in as many games.

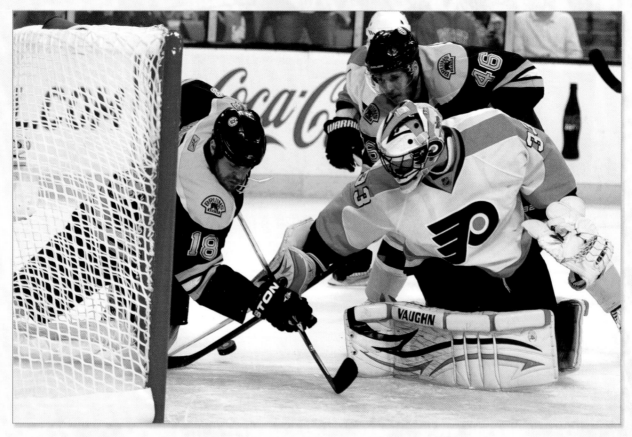

Nathan Horton (left) and David Krejci try to stop goalie Brian Boucher from making a save.

48

Conference Semi-Final — Boston Bruins vs. Philadelphia Flyers

Giant captain Zdeno Chara celebrates a goal with the smaller Brad Marchand.

Conference Semi-Final — Boston Bruins vs. Philadelphia Flyers

49

Goalie Brian Boucher tries to follow play through a scrum of players in front of his crease.

Andrej Meszaros got the only Flyers' goal late in the period, but they could get no closer. Boston got the only goal of the third, a late marker on the power play from Chara, on another slapper. This marked the first man-advantage goal by the Bruins this playoff year after a 0-for-30 drought. Coming on a five-on-three, it emphasized a dominating performance by the Bruins in front of their home fans, and gave the team a huge lead in the series.

"We learned last year that the fourth win is the hardest," said Thomas who, like his teammates, spoke from experience. "We are playing one game at a time,

one period at a time, and one shift at a time. We are going to try to play it the same way come Friday."

For Philadelphia coach Peter Laviolette, the task ahead was much simpler. "I'll throw a whole bunch cliches at you, one game at a time, one day at a time, one period at a time," he began. "That's really all we can think about. We can't think about winning four in row. We can't think of any of that stuff, we just have to come and play the way we know we can and keep getting traffic and win a period, and hopefully win a game, and get to Game five."

50

Conference Semi-Final — Boston Bruins vs. Philadelphia Flyers

GAME FOUR — *May 6, 2011*

Philadelphia 1 at **Boston 5**

*(**Boston** wins series 4–0)*

Milan Lucic scored his first two goals in twenty games, and the Boston Bruins took a close game and made it lop-sided by scoring the only four goals of the third period en route to eliminating Philadelphia in four straight games. It was sweet revenge for 2010, when the Flyers rallied to win in seven, and the win set up a Conference Final against Tampa Bay. It marked the first time since 1992 that the Bruins had advanced that far.

"It's been kind of frustrating, the last twenty games, not being able to put the puck in the back of the net," Lucic confessed. "But tonight I was able to get open, and when I got those opportunities, both great plays by (Nathan) Horton to set me up, and when I got the opportunities it was nice to step up and score big goals."

The Flyers, who in recent years have had Stanley Cup-quality teams but with shaky goaltending, battled more demons this night as coach Peter Laviolette started Sergei Bobrovsky for the first time in the series after he had appeared in relief in each of the first three games. He and Brian Boucher had had great stretches during the season, and other stretches of weak or inconsistent play, making choosing a number-one goalie a moving target for Laviolette. Tonight, he tried Bobrovsky, but it was no more successful than Boucher in the first three games.

Lucic got the only goal of the first period on a power play, the second straight man-advantage goal of the Bruins after a 0-for-30 skein, but the Flyers tied the

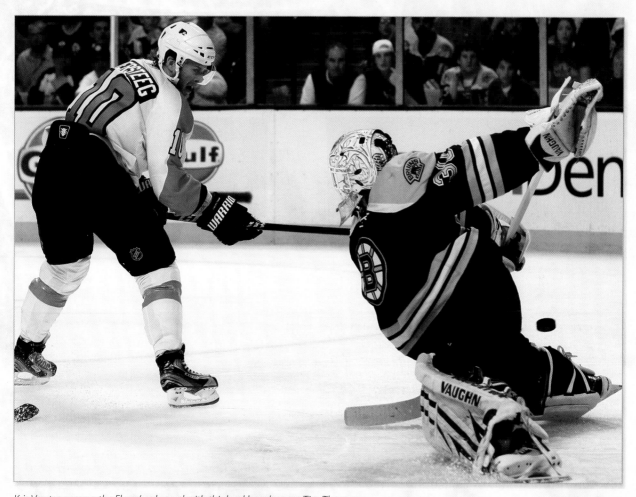

Kris Versteeg scores the Flyers' only goal with this backhander past Tim Thomas.

Conference Semi-Final — Boston Bruins vs. Philadelphia Flyers

51

Mike Richards of the Flyers is upended by Dennis Seidenberg in front of the Boston goal while Tim Thomas smothers the puck.

Scott Hartnell and Zdeno Chara shake hands after the Bruins completed a four-game sweep of the Flyers.

game at 13:22 of the second when Kris Versteeg stole the puck from Brad Marchand and beat Tim Thomas with a backhand.

Buoyed by this turn of events, the Flyers came out strong to start the third, but their energy was suffused by a routine point shot from Johnny Boychuk that was flubbed by Bobrovsky. This got the Bruins on track and they rattled off three more goals to close out the win. Lucic got his second of the game with just under five minutes to play on a breakaway. Marchand and Daniel Paille scored empty-net goals as the Flyers pulled out all stops to get back into the game.

"To be honest, I'm glad that it's over," said goalie Thomas. "I'm glad that it's done with because the longer that series would have went the more talk about last year. So, I'm glad that is put behind us as

a team, as an organization, and the fans. I am glad the fans can put it behind them, too. And I'll say it, hopefully we exorcised some demons."

Offered Philadelphia captain Mike Richards: "I'm not sure where it went wrong. It's a slippery slope when you stop playing your brand of hockey. Give the Bruins a lot of credit. They played extremely well. We just didn't have an answer for it."

Indeed, the Flyers were outplayed in all aspects of the game, not just the scoreboard. The Bruins blocked more shots as a team and were vastly superior in the faceoff circle, and Thomas was reliable, steady, and superior to his Philadelphia counterparts. The Bruins played with greater emotion and executed when they had to, and as a result, they advanced and the Flyers went home for the summer.

Conference Semi-Final — Boston Bruins vs. Philadelphia Flyers

53

STANLEY CUP PLAYOFFS 2011

GAME ONE — *May 14, 2011*

Tampa Bay 5 at Boston 2
(Tampa Bay leads series 1-0)

It would have been impossible to predict what might happen in this game prior to the opening faceoff. Tampa Bay, after all, had swept by Washington in four games and had a nine-day vacation, while the Bruins swept Philly and had eight days off. Both teams were hot, but now rusty.

No one could have predicted, though, that a tense opening half of the first period of the series would explode with three Lightning goals in a minute and a half. It was enough of a burst to send the Bruins reeling and give Tampa its eighth straight win of the 2011 playoffs.

"We wanted to come out and play our game and I think we did that," said star Tampa Bay forward Martin St. Louis. "I thought they came out hard, especially the first three or four minutes. I thought they were skating

Brad Marchand looks to move the puck in front while goalie Dwayne Roloson follows the play.

54

Conference Final — Boston Bruins vs. Tampa Bay Lightning

Boston's Dennis Seidenberg crowds the crease while Steve Stamkos (left) and goalie Dwayne Roloson watch him closely.

really hard and making good plays in the neutral zone. But we didn't get spooked by it. We just kept going at it, kept skating, got our forecheck going a little bit and created some chances. We were opportunistic on those and, obviously, it's a lot easier to play with the lead in this league than trying to chase."

Sean Bergenheim started the quick strikes when he took advantage of two turnovers in the Boston end and snapped a loose puck past Tim Thomas at 11:15 for the first goal of the series. Just nineteen seconds

later, Brett Clark made a Bobby Orr-like dash from his end, finishing with a nice backhand which Thomas couldn't find in time. And then, at 12:40, Teddy Purcell scored on another backhand, making it 3–0 and forcing Claude Julien to call a timeout and restore order to his Bruins' psyche.

"It's a tough hole to get out of," Thomas confessed. "Two would have been better. I was thinking, when we went down 2–0, I was thinking I was going to make this like Philly game two, I'm just going to hold them

Conference Final — Boston Bruins vs. Tampa Bay Lightning

55

Goalie Tim Thomas makes a glove save, much to the disappointment of Teddy Purcell (#16).

to two, and we'll come back and win this game. But the third goal was a surprise, you know, bad-bounce goal, and that made it more difficult. But having said that, it was 3–1 in the second period, and if we could've won one period at a time, we're still in that game."

It was 3–1 courtesy of Tyler Seguin. Playing his first game of the playoffs after being a healthy scratch for eleven games, he was inserted into the lineup after Patrice Bergeron suffered a concussion in the previous game. His quick shot fooled Dwayne Roloson, but any thoughts of the goal sparking a comeback were thwarted by the Lightning when Marc-Andre Bergeron got a power-play goal at 13:37 of the third.

Simon Gagne then scored into the empty net to make it 5–1, and Johnny Boychuk scored a more or less meaningless goal at 18:59 to close out the scoring.

Tampa Bay coach Guy Boucher knew his team couldn't take its foot off the pedal, though, despite the terrific road win to start the series. "They're a really good team," he said. "They came out hard. They're going to come out harder the next game. I'm expecting Bergeron to be in the lineup. I know Tim Thomas is going to make miracles. I'll be shocked if he doesn't come out with his best game of the playoffs. They got a lot of pride. They came back in the first series from two games. I mean, it's only one game. We've done nothing yet."

56

Conference Final — Boston Bruins vs. Tampa Bay Lightning

GAME TWO — *May 17, 2011*

Tampa Bay 5 at **Boston 6**

(series tied 1-1)

If this wasn't one of the most entertaining playoff games in the last decade, what one was? For whatever reason, whatever was in the air or water around the TD Garden, both teams threw away the playbook and played wide-open shinny, scoring eleven goals and providing fans of both teams with as many thrills and chills as one night could handle. There were three lead changes, a wild comeback that fell just short, and one of the greatest rookie playoff games ever. More important for the Bruins, their 6–5 win tied the series 1–1 as the venue shifted to Florida for two games.

Tyler Seguin, playing his second straight game after being a healthy scratch for the first eleven games, had two goals and two assists in the second period, keying a rally that saw Boston outscore the Lightning 5–1 in the middle twenty minutes. It was a bravura performance for Seguin, the second overall selection at the 2010 Entry Draft.

Goalie Dwayne Roloson makes the save and then averts his head from the oncoming spray created by players sliding to a fast stop.

Conference Final — Boston Bruins vs. Tampa Bay Lightning

57

Big Zdeno Chara does two things at once, checking Steve Stamkos along the boards while trying to prevent Martin St. Louis from controlling the puck.

Lost in his great night was the one goal, three assist night from Tampa Bay's Vincent Lecavalier.

"I felt more confident, more poised, and in big games I always want to step up," said the nineteen-year-old Seguin. "Tonight, I had some lucky bounces, but I was trying to take advantage of all opportunities, and they were going in tonight."

Lucky for the Bruins he came up big when he did. Tampa Bay took it to the Bruins again in the first period, picking up where it left off in game one. Adam Hall stunned the Boston crowd with a goal just thirteen seconds after the opening faceoff on the first rush of the game, and it was the Lightning that kept coming at the stunned Bruins.

Fortunately, Nathan Horton clicked on a power play midway through the period with Hall in the box for roughing, but Martin St. Louis scored with just seven seconds left in the period off a sensational play from linemate Steve Stamkos. Stamkos barreled down the right wing and turned away from the goal, but he pulled a Sidney Crosby play by backhanding a pass to St. Louis in front. St. Louis then made a sensational little deflection that caught Thomas off guard, and the Lightning went to the dressing room with a huge psychological advantage.

Then Seguin went to work. In the first minute of the second period he took a pass from Michael Ryder as he flew through the centre-ice area, split the

58

Conference Final — Boston Bruins vs. Tampa Bay Lightning

defencemen and roofed a backhander over a sprawled Thomas. Seguin's speed was awesome to watch, and the goal lifted the fans from their seats. Less than two minutes later, David Krejci gave the Bruins their first lead of the series on a nice deflection, and Seguin got his second when he snapped a wicked shot over Dwayne Roloson's glove.

Vincent Lecavalier got one back for Tampa Bay to make it a 4–3 game, but the Bruins kept pressing and scored two goals later in the period from Ryder. The first came on the power play on a setup by Seguin, and the second, at 19:41, made it 6–3.

That spelled the end for forty-one-year-old Roloson, who was replaced by Mike Smith for the third.

But nothing was normal on this night, and a three-goal Bruins lead with twenty minutes to play was not a sure thing. Stamkos got an early goal to make it 6–4 and give Tampa Bay a little hope, and then Dominic Moore scored at 13:15 to make it 6–5. A frenetic pace at the end wasn't enough, and Thomas held the Bruins in there long enough to escape with the thrilling victory.

But at the end of the night, all conversation focused on Seguin. "I think it was his first goal, he went up the ice, just flying, and that was a nice goal," said Lecavalier. "He was skating hard. He is a great skater. He is a smart player. The first two games for him have been great. We definitely have to keep an eye on him and make sure the structure we play is better and not give those chances."

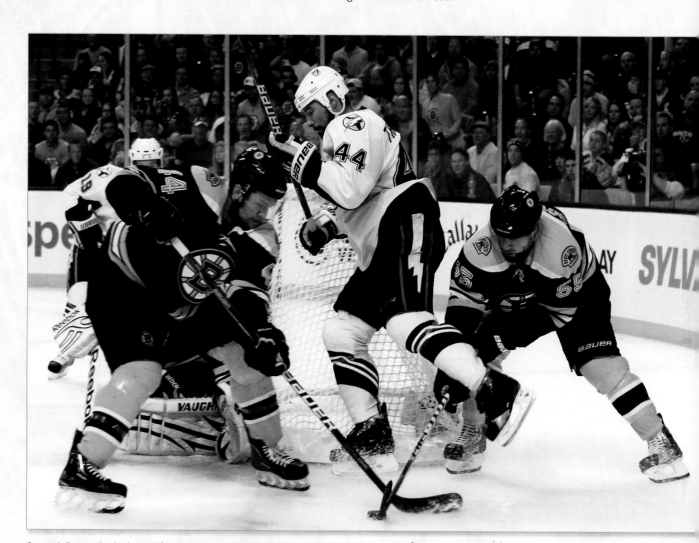

Boston's Dennis Seidenberg (left) and Johnny Boychuk double their efforts to check Nate Thompson off the puck.

GAME THREE — *May 19, 2011*

Boston 2 at Tampa Bay 0

(Boston leads series 2-1)

"That felt more like a normal game. That felt like the game we played most of the season. That was Boston Bruins hockey."

So said Bruins goalie Tim Thomas after stopping thirty-one shots and earning his first shutout of the 2011 playoffs in a 2–0 win over Tampa Bay at the St. Pete Times Forum. The win returned home-ice advantage in the series to Boston and was impressive for the team's superior play in all aspects of the game.

Key to the victory was a superb goal from David Krejci just sixty-nine seconds into the game. It silenced the crowd, got his own team revved up, and allowed the Bruins to dictate play. He was left unattended and linemate Milan Lucic threw a blind pass to the slot hoping to hit his own man. Krejci did the rest, undressing Dwayne Roloson for his seventh goal of the playoffs. It stood up as the game winner, his fourth of the playoffs.

"It was a great pass by Lucic," said Krejci. "I don't know how he saw me."

The goal changed the tenor of the game. The Bruins stuck with their game of blocking shots, clogging the middle in their own end to keep shooters to the outside,

A diving Victor Hedman knocks the puck off the stick of Mark Recchi.

Tim Thomas dives out to make a sprawling save and cover up the puck.

A goalie's view shows Tim Thomas making the save while teammate Zdeno Chara checks Martin St. Louis.

and staying out of the penalty box. They had only four minors, but one was off-setting. Of course, they were flawless on the penalty kill, and although Thomas had thirty-one shots to only twenty-five for Roloson, most were not dangerous, quality scoring chances.

Adding to the cause was the return of Patrice Bergeron, who missed the first two games of the series with a concussion. "I really liked the way he played," Boston coach Claude Julien opined. "Obviously, you see the difference he can make for our hockey club faceoff-wise, but also his responsibility at both ends of the ice."

It was a difference the Lightning weren't able to match. "Offensively, I don't feel like we paid the price," suggested Tampa Bay forward Martin St. Louis. "I think we have done that in the past couple of games…We just didn't get the job done."

While Tampa Bay was met with stifling team defence, the Bruins got a huge goal at 8:12 of the third to pad their lead. Andrew Ference took a point shot off a great shift of cycling by the Bruins, and the puck made its way through a screen of players, through Roloson's pads, and trickled over the blue-line.

Soon after Tampa Bay had a power play when captain Zdeno Chara was called for hooking, but the Bruins penalty killers stood tall and denied the Lightning any chance of getting back into the game.

62

Conference Final — Boston Bruins vs. Tampa Bay Lightning

GAME FOUR — *May 21, 2011*

Boston 3 at **Tampa Bay 5**

(series tied 2-2)

Perspective is everything in sports. Tonight's game, for instance. For Boston fans, it was a huge opportunity wasted. For Tampa Bay fans, well, what a comeback—what a comeback!

The Bruins took control of the game, and the series, with three unanswered goals in the first period, only to blow the lead over the last forty minutes. Instead of going home with a 3–1 lead in games, it was now 2–2, meaning teams were now playing a best-of-three.

Teddy Purcell and Simon Gagne were the heroes for the Lightning while the entire defensive effort of Boston was sent to the doghouse after the game. "We just lost our focus," Bruins coach Claude Julien admitted in measured tones. "We played really well in the first period, not because of what the score was, but because we did the right things and we took that lead. The message was pretty clear; we had to continue playing the same way."

That way started with a goal from Patrice Bergeron who capitalized on a Victor Hedman turnover behind the Lightning goal. He intercepted a Hedman pass intended for Chris Clark and walked out front where

Mark Recchi (left) and Mattias Ohlund battle to the side of the Tampa Bay goal.

Conference Final — Boston Bruins vs. Tampa Bay Lightning

63

Goalie Mike Smith was perfect in his relief appearance, stopping everything including this chance from Zdeno Chara.

64

Conference Final — Boston Bruins vs. Tampa Bay Lightning

It wasn't the Bruins' night as Tampa Bay rallied with five unanswered goals for the win.

he stuffed it in behind Dwayne Roloson at 11:47. Five minutes later, Michael Ryder got his fifth goal of the playoffs on a lucky play. Skating down the left wing on a two-on-one, he passed the puck across the crease and it went off the stick of defenceman Mike Lundin and past Roloson, who had no chance to reverse his movement.

Bergeron got his second of the period short-handed. The Lightning gave the puck up at the Boston blue-line and Bergeron walked in off the rush, beating Roloson between the pads from the faceoff circle. That goal spelled the end for the goalie, who was replaced for the second time in three games by Mike Smith. Smith was excellent the rest of the way, giving up nary a goal or even rebound.

The Bruins headed to the dressing room with a 3–0 lead thanks to sensational play, but the Lightning started the second period in kind. And it was under-valued Teddy Purcell who keyed the comeback which saw Tampa Bay score three times in four minutes, early in the period. Purcell got his first at 6:55 after Zdeno Chara coughed the puck up behind his net. It came out front and Purcell's quick backhand eluded Tim Thomas.

Just sixty-three seconds later, Purcell was back at it. He ripped a hard shot from the top of the circle after taking a perfect set-up from Mattias Ohlund at the point. And then Sean Bergenheim completed the comeback, stealing the puck from Tomas Kaberle behind the Bruins goal and coming out front to beat Thomas at 10:58.

Although the game was still tied, the Bruins were reeling. Tampa Bay had settled down thanks to Smith in goal, and it had all the momentum to start the third. Gagne got the go-ahead goal at 6:54 on a bit of a lucky play. Ryan Malone intercepted the puck at the blue-line and brought the puck down the right side, and his shot bounced off Dennis Seidenberg's skate right to Gagne, who made no mistake with half a net to shoot at.

Martin St. Louis closed out the scoring with an empty netter, but the story of the night was the comeback. A certain Boston win became a loss in the blink of an eye.

"We knew we could do it," Lightning coach Guy Boucher said. "We've been extremely resilient. We came back so many times this year, and everyone knows that in the third period we keep coming and coming."

The feeling in the other dressing room was quite different. "When you're up, you almost sit back a bit," Boston's Brad Marchand admitted. "You think that the game is over, and that's what we did. We thought that we had them."

Nope. Not tonight.

Conference Final — Boston Bruins vs. Tampa Bay Lightning

65

GAME FIVE — May 23, 2011

Tampa Bay 1 at Boston 3
(Boston leads series 3-2)

Offering a vintage goaltending performance, Boston's Tim Thomas almost single-handedly gave his team a 3–1 win in game five to put the Bruins a single win away from a trip back to the Stanley Cup Final for the first time since 1990, while the rest of the team got off to a surprisingly sluggish start in such a critical game on home ice.

"Against this goaltender, you need more. You need more," a stunned Lightning coach Guy Boucher said of Thomas. "You need miracles. He is making miracles. We have to come up with miracles."

"It's unbelievable some of the saves that Timmy makes," said Bruins teammate Chris Kelly. "He's a pleasure to have. I think every guy in this room cannot say enough good things about him."

Most of the talk after the game was about one save in particular. Leading 2–1 midway through the third period, the Bruins were on their heels. Eric Brewer fired a point shot that Thomas came out to challenge, but the puck went wide, bounced back in front and onto the stick of Steve Downie. He shot the puck into the open net, but Thomas lunged back and got the blade of his stick on the puck millimeters from the goal line.

Simon Gagne got the only goal of the opening period to stake Tampa Bay to a 1–0 lead, just sixty-nine seconds into the game at that, but the Lightning were such the better team in the period that the Bruins actually felt pretty good in the dressing room, knowing that they were down only a goal and Thomas playing so well.

Meanwhile, at the other end, changes were significant. Boucher decided to start backup goalie Mike Smith and give Dwayne Roloson the night off.

Boston's Michael Ryder and Ryan Malone chase after a loose puck.

In his customary celebratory gesture after victory, Tim Thomas expresses the joy and relief of another playoff win.

The forty-one-year-old Roloson had had his erratic moments in the series, and Smith had a long and impressive stint in relief the previous game to earn the start. He was perfect in the opening period, but had to face only four shots, a situation that changed dramatically in the second.

The Bruins tied the game early in the second period on a great series of passes by the Nathan Horton–David Krejci–Milan Lucic line, Horton finishing the play with a great snap shot that Smith had little chance on.

The Bruins got the go-ahead goal late in the second when Brad Marchand deftly redirected a Patrice Bergeron pass at 15:56. Try as they might, Tampa Bay couldn't get the tying goal and Rich Peverley added an empty netter in the final minute.

"We're happy with the win, but you haven't accomplished anything with a 3–2 [series] lead," Bergeron suggested. "Obviously, we need that fourth win and it's the toughest one to get. And we know they're not going to quit, and, for us, it's about finding a way."

Incredibly, the Bruins were managing to win games through five-on-five hockey, their power play continuing to struggle but their penalty killing virtually perfect as well. Tonight, they allowed only three power plays against but were also 0-for-3 with their own man advantage opportunities.

Conference Final — Boston Bruins vs. Tampa Bay Lightning

67

GAME SIX — *May 25, 2011*

Boston 4 at **Tampa Bay 5**

(series tied 3-3)

Dwayne Roloson was back in goal for the Lightning and the big three of Steve Stamkos, Vincent Lecavalier, and Martin St. Louis had their biggest game of the series when it mattered most. Lecavalier had two assists; St. Louis had two goals and an assist; and Stamkos had a goal and two assists. Tampa had a lead, lost it, claimed it back, and almost lost it again. The heart-stopping game forced a deciding seventh in the series.

"I was expecting a big game from those guys," Lightning coach Guy Boucher admitted. "I disagree that they didn't have big games in the last games. There's a lot more in the game than scoring goals and having points. They had very good games before; it just wasn't going in for some of them."

As much as they had a big game on ice, they also had an impact in the dressing room, as Steve Stamkos acknowledged. "He's the heart and soul of our team," Stamkos said of linemate and scoring sensation St. Louis. "He and Vinny are our leaders. You see how hard Marty works during the game. You guys get to see that but you don't see what happens in the room. He's the first guy to step up and get the guys going. He's obviously been through every type of experience and every single type of championship you could win, he's been there. He's won individual awards. He's won the Stanley Cup and he's always been a big part. He knows what to do and how to react in those situations. And he stepped up before the game and said a few words,

Boston captain Zdeno Chara is not easily slowed down, but this time goalie Dwayne Roloson kicks the puck out of harm's way.

68

Conference Final — Boston Bruins vs. Tampa Bay Lightning

Tampa Bay's Steve Downie makes a great pass out of the reach of Tim Thomas to a teammate going to the net.

and just the respect he has from every single guy on the team. Coming from him, we take that to heart."

However, as much as the top players were a factor, special teams also played a role. The Lighting had three power-play goals while the Bruins had only one.

The hot Teddy Purcell also chipped in with two more goals, including the first of the game just thirty-six seconds into the opening period. It came off a clever play by Lecavalier at the faceoff circle deep in the Boston end.

"I saw it wasn't their first centerman," Lecavalier explained of how the play began. "He got kicked off and [Kelly] coming in as a lefty, I knew if I won it, it would go between my legs. I just gave him [Purcell] a little wink and told him to move over. I got lucky and it ended up going right on his stick."

Undaunted, the Bruins took control of the rest of the period and scored twice. Milan Lucic counted goals at 7:09 and at 16:30 David Krejci had his eighth of the playoffs and first of three on the night.

But just as the Bruins had gained confidence and looked like they might end the series tonight, the home side wasn't prepared to go into the summer just yet. St. Louis and Purcell both tallied with the extra man in the second period, and now the Lightning had the lead with just twenty minutes left.

They increased their lead thirty-four seconds into the third thanks to Stamkos, also on the power play. Krejci responded with the Bruins' only power play goal, and then St. Louis got his tenth of the playoffs. Krejci got his hat-trick goal at 13:28, also his tenth, to tie St. Louis for the playoff lead, but the Bruins could get no closer. Tampa Bay's big guns stepped up and held the fort.

And so game seven was needed with plenty of storylines to accompany it. Special teams and goaltending were factors, as was pressure and home ice and performances coming from the big stars. But the consequences were huge. Winner goes to the Stanley Cup Final; losers look back all summer at what might have been.

Tampa Bay's Martin St. Louis drives toward the net on his backhand.

70

Conference Final — Boston Bruins vs. Tampa Bay Lightning

GAME SEVEN — *May 27, 2011*

Tampa Bay 0 at **Boston 1**

(Boston wins series 4-3)

Sometimes a 1–0 hockey game reflects boring and defensive hockey dominated by the trap, chipping and chasing, anything but skill. This game seven was just the opposite; a classic game one might normally associate with the great Original Six battles.

"That was as close to a perfect game seven as you are going to get," said Boston's star of the crease, Tim Thomas. His teammate, defenceman Andrew Ference, agreed in spades.

"We have been waiting for that sixty-minute game, and that was it, man. We had a good start, a good middle, and we just kind of kept it up. I was impressed. It was a heart-stopper because it was so close. Both sides played well. It was a great game seven. Persistence paid off."

And much as the players contributed to the high quality of the game, veteran referees Stephen Walkom and Dan O'Halloran also deserve credit.

Collapsing around their goalie, four Bruins help Tim Thomas deal with Tampa Bay pressure.

Conference Final — Boston Bruins vs. Tampa Bay Lightning

71

They called not a single penalty all game, letting the players decide which team was better. And all players responded by avoiding scrums after whistles, diving, and whatever else might have given the refs reason to dish out penalties.

Nathan Horton was the hero of the night, and he made history in the process, becoming the first player in Stanley Cup history to score two game-winning, game seven goals in one year. It was a great goal and the culmination of a great game, one featuring plenty of scoring chances, great goaltending, and a world-class goal.

On the winning play, David Krejci came down the left wing and watched as teammate Nathan Horton skated full bore to the front of the net. Krejci waited for the moment Horton was nearly on top of goalie Dwayne Roloson and then fired a hard pass that Horton merely had to get his stick on to direct it into the goal.

"I just tried to drive the net and I just went with my stick on the ice," Horton explained. "He's such a good player and a good passer and such a smart hockey player. He just passed it to me, and it just hit my stick and went in."

It was a fast and precise strike at 12:27 of the third period, and Tampa Bay had no answer for it. Tim Thomas closed the door on the Lightning, stopping all twenty-four shots and earning his second shutout

Martin St. Louis (left) and Zdeno Chara: two great stars of greatly differing heights share mutual admiration.

Conference champions Boston Bruins celebrate their seven-game victory over Tampa Bay in one of the more exciting playoff series in recent years.

of the series. But to be fair, the Bruins were the better team excepting Roloson, who was the best player on either side. He was just one perfect shot shy of a shutout of his own, or of at least forcing overtime.

Indeed, almost from the drop of the puck overtime seemed to be looming. Teams were sensational in their own end despite the many scoring chances, but time and again Roloson gave his team a chance to win on enemy ice. He had a perfect record of 7–0

in elimination games in his career, including 4–0 this year, but he couldn't get to 8–0.

The Bruins were off to the Stanley Cup Final, but the Lightning had had a sensational season under rookie GM Steve Yzerman and first-year coach Guy Boucher. The Lightning will be back this deep in the playoffs soon and often. The Bruins? They had a date with the Vancouver Canucks for the Dominion Challenge Trophy, aka the Stanley Cup.

Conference Final — Boston Bruins vs. Tampa Bay Lightning

73

GAME ONE — *June 1, 2011*

Boston 0 at **Vancouver 1**
(Vancouver leads series 1-0)

The Boston Bruins began the Cup Final with a nearly flawless road show, taking the crowd out of the game and presenting the Canucks with solid team defence for all but about five seconds of the game. But in that stretch, Raffi Torres was the hero for Vancouver, scoring a dramatic goal with only 18.5 seconds left on the clock when overtime seemed a certainty. The goal broke down into three moments.

First, Ryan Kesler beat Johnny Boychuk to the puck at the Boston blue-line, got the puck over the line and stayed onside. Then, he fired a cross-ice pass to winger Jannik Hansen, who had moved in on the play. Hansen then waited until big defenceman Zdeno Chara fell to the ice trying to block either a pass or shot, managing to get the puck to Torres streaking to the goal.

Torres then got his stick down and re-directed the hard pass beyond the reach of goalie Tim Thomas, who had been the best player for either side all night. A sloppy but thrilling opening game ended with a victory for the Canucks, and two of the goalies nominated for the Vezina Trophy were their team's best players all night.

"He [Hansen] got himself into a position where I started respecting the shot and started to cut down

Vancouver's Ryan Kesler and Boston captain Zdeno Chara go toe-to-toe in front of the Bruins goal.

74

Stanley Cup Final — Boston Bruins vs. Vancouver Canucks

the angle," Thomas described. "He was able to pass it to the guy (Torres) who was cutting to the net, who I didn't even see was there."

Hansen had been stoned five minutes into the third period by Thomas on a clear breakaway as he chose to put the puck between the goalie's legs only to have Thomas get down low and make the critical save.

The game could be divided into two distinct parts— the first two periods and the third period. In the first part, teams exchanged a seemingly countless number of penalties, yet neither side could score. For Boston, the power play drought continued as it went 0–for–6, that part of the game being the team's weakest all playoffs. But for the Canucks, the man advantage had

Daniel Sedin leaps out of the way as goalie Tim Thomas makes a save.

Stanley Cup Final — Boston Bruins vs. Vancouver Canucks

75

Raffi Torres redirects a perfect pass from Jannik Hansen with just 18.5 seconds left in regulation to give the Canucks a 1-0 win.

been a sizeable bonus for eighteen games, so their inability to score was surprising.

In the third period, though, the referees put away their whistles and didn't call a single minor after signaling thirteen in the first forty minutes. And the Canucks dominated play, time and again, creating great chances but just unable to beat Thomas, who sparkled in the Boston cage. It seemed only a matter of time before they would score, but as the clock sped towards 0:00, it also looked more certain that the game would go to overtime. And then Kesler started the game-deciding play.

"Obviously, in the third period they were the better team, and they ended up scoring that goal," admitted Boston coach Claude Julien. "It got away from us, but we still got an opportunity here in the next game to hopefully get that one and kind of get the home-ice advantage."

At the other end, Luongo was equally reliable when needed, and as the game went on it became clear the first goal wouldn't just be a big goal—it would likely be the game winner. Incredibly, though, Luongo had now won the first game of the last eight playoff series in which he played.

76

Stanley Cup Final — Boston Bruins vs. Vancouver Canucks

GAME TWO — *June 4, 2011*

Boston 2 at **Vancouver 3**
(Vancouver leads series 2-0)

The Bruins lost the first two games at home to Montreal to start the playoffs, and now they were in a similar corner after giving up a late goal in regulation and another in sudden-death overtime. The 3-2 win gave Vancouver a 2-0 series lead, and that lead was due largely to Alexandre Burrows who had two goals and an assist including the OT winner.

It was his third OT winner in 2011 and came close to the all-time record for fastest overtime goal, set by Montreal's Brian Skrudland in 1986 against Calgary. The goal put Burrows in rare and exclusive company, for only Mel Hill in 1939 and Maurice Richard in 1951 have scored three extra-time winners in one playoff year (Hill got all of his in one series, no less).

It was a game that at times was strategically defensive and at other times wide open, as teams exchanged glorious scoring chances. As in game one, the goalies were as much of the story as any of the skaters, but tonight it was the gambling style of Boston's Tim Thomas that cost the team a win. On the winning goal, Burrows skated down the left wing, faked a shot to draw Thomas way out of the net, and then wrapped the puck around and in from the far side. Thomas, known to come well out to challenge shooters, lost out on this play, but it's a style that has worked well for him throughout his renaissance.

"I know Tim Thomas likes to challenge," Burrows explained. "If I shoot there, I think he stops it. So I wanted to walk around and shoot it right away but he tripped me and I lost the puck a little bit. I was lucky enough just to be able to wrap it."

The Bruins had the same lineup as game one, but Vancouver coach Alain Vigneault made two changes. First, he inserted Andrew Alberts for Dan Hamhuis, who was injured in the series opener, and then he

Goalie Roberto Luongo makes a pad save while Milan Lucic tries to cause a distraction in front.

Stanley Cup Final — Boston Bruins vs. Vancouver Canucks

77

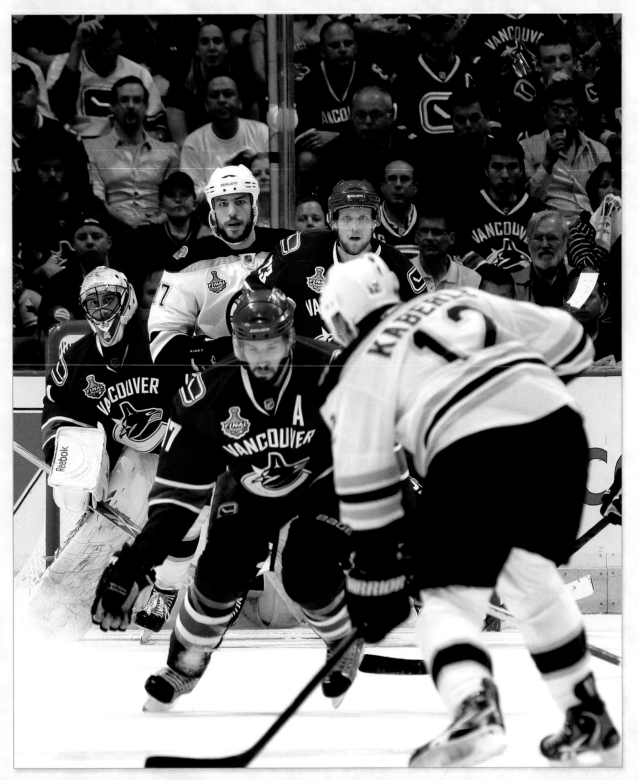

Tomas Kaberle takes a slapshot as Ryan Kesler tries to block it. Goalie Roberto Luongo struggles to see the puck through traffic.

78

Stanley Cup Final — Boston Bruins vs. Vancouver Canucks

Alexandre Burrows starts the play that leads to the OT winner, faking goalie Tim Thomas and going behind the net.

gave Manny Malhotra his first start since mid-March when Malhotra suffered a serious eye injury.

Burrows got the only goal of the first period on a power play after Zdeno Chara was called for interference on Ryan Kesler. It was his eighth goal of the playoffs but first with the extra man, and it came on a quick shot that Thomas wasn't expecting. The play was set up thanks to a beautiful touch pass from Chris Higgins, and Burrows's shot snuck under the blocker arm of Thomas.

Boston, sensing the urgency of the game, came out and played its best period of the series in the second, scoring twice and dominating play. Milan Lucic tied the game on a Boston power play, sliding a rebound under Luongo, and then Mark Recchi scored a beautiful goal when he redirected a quick Chara point shot while drifting through the slot.

But the Canucks took the play to Boston in the third while the Bruins tried to nurse the lead. Thomas had to make several good saves, but time and again he came out well beyond the blue ice to cut down the angle. This proved costly on the tying goal. A quick point shot from Alexander Edler was deflected by Daniel Sedin in front, but it ended up on Burrows's

stick. He dished the puck off to Sedin again, and while Thomas was splayed out on the ice five feet from his goal line, Sedin snapped the puck in the empty net.

"I think that comes from him knowing where we're going to be and we know where he's going to be," said Henrik Sedin of Burrows. "In those areas, he looks up and knows Danny is going to come there. That comes from playing together for a long time. He made a great play there."

That set the stage for Burrows's incredibly quick OT winner, propelling Vancouver into a commanding lead in the series. It was Boston's first overtime loss during these playoffs after four straight wins while the Canucks improved to 4–2. As well, Boston had been 6–0 when leading after forty minutes, but that perfect record, too, now had a blemish thanks to Burrows.

Great as Vancouver's start to the series had been, though, Burrows cautioned against over-enthusiasm. "We haven't won anything yet," he noted. "It's only two games. We've only taken care of home ice. They're a really good team and I'm sure they're going to feed off the energy from their crowd. We have to make sure we're ready to go in there. It won't be easy. Until you win a road game, you're not in control of any series."

Stanley Cup Final — Boston Bruins vs. Vancouver Canucks

79

GAME THREE — *June 6, 2011*

Vancouver 1 at **Boston 8**
(Vancouver leads series 2-1)

Well, no one predicted a sweep, and a sweep was not in the cards after the Bruins opened a huge lead in the second period and rolled to a one-sided win in game three. It was, in truth, a must-win game for the Bruins because to have lost would have meant being 3–0 down in the series. Only once in Stanley Cup Final history has a team overcome such a deficit to win, and that was in 1942 (Toronto).

"This team has done that in the past when it was tested and I think we did it again tonight, "said Andrew Ference. "It wasn't pretty. It was Boston hockey."

The victory was fuelled by, of all things, special teams, that part of the game that had been the Bruins' greatest nemesis all playoffs long. More to the point, the Bruins scored two power-play goals and two short-handed goals, taking a scoreless game after twenty minutes and turning it into a rout by the end of the second period.

But perhaps the most important moment in the game came early in the first period. Boston's Nathan

Vancouver's Chris Higgins is stopped point blank by Tim Thomas while defenceman Zdeno Chara looks on.

80

Stanley Cup Final — Boston Bruins vs. Vancouver Canucks

Henrik Sedin goes to the net only to be checked by goalie Tim Thomas who plays the body and ignores the puck.

Horton was the victim of a head shot from Aaron Rome after making a pass just inside the Vancouver blue-line. Rome was given a five-minute major for interference and a game misconduct, and Horton was carried off on a stretcher. Boston didn't capitalize on the long power play, and Horton, of course, didn't return for the rest of the game, but the Bruins drew inspiration from the play and took it to the Canucks in the second period.

"It is so tough when you see a guy go down like that," said Brad Marchand. "You are so worried about him. We're all so close in this room and we care about Horty a lot. It played on our mind in the rest of the first period, but we were able to use it to our advantage after that."

Just as eleven seconds was huge in game two, the time that Alexandre Burrows scored in overtime to give Vancouver a 3–2 win, so, too, was it big this night. Just eleven seconds into the second period Andrew Ference blew a slapshot past Roberto Luongo to give the home side a 1–0 lead, a lead they never relinquished. Four minutes later, forty-three-year-old Mark Recchi scored on the power play, although this time he merely got credit for a goal redirected accidentally by Vancouver's Ryan Kesler past Luongo.

The killer came midway through the period when Marchand converted a short-handed chance. He beat the Vancouver defence on a rush, and as he slid across the crease and outwaited the falling, sprawling

Stanley Cup Final — Boston Bruins vs. Vancouver Canucks

81

Boston's David Krejci celebrates his second-period goal to give his team a commanding 4-0 lead.

Luongo he roofed a shot to make it 3–0, more or less sealing the victory in the process. David Krejci scored his eleventh playoff goal late in the period to make it 4–0, and in the third Tim Thomas held the fort as Vancouver tried in vain to get back into the game.

"All of a sudden, it was like the wheels fell off a bit and everything was going their way," offered Luongo. "You know, obviously, it's one of those games where we are all disappointed with the result. But, at the end of the day, a loss is a loss."

Daniel Paille got the second short-handed goal of the game midway through the final period when his shot squirted under the glove arm of Luongo, and Jannik Hansen's goal merely ended Thomas's shutout. Boston tallied three late goals in a game in which everything and anything it put on net went in.

For Boston, it had to keep this fortuitous scoring going another game, and for the Canucks, they had to erase this result from their memory. After all, a win in game four would allow them to go home and win the Cup two nights later at their own Rogers Arena. A loss would tie the series and make the outcome of the Stanley Cup Final entirely up in the air.

82

Stanley Cup Final — Boston Bruins vs. Vancouver Canucks

GAME FOUR — *June 8, 2011*

Vancouver 0 at **Boston 4**
(series tied 2–2)

The Boston Bruins finished their mini home stand by doing exactly what Vancouver had done—winning the two games on their own ice. They did so with another emphatic victory, making for an interesting lead-up to game five. Vancouver had home-ice advantage still in what was now a best-of-three series, but the Bruins had all the momentum.

Again, it was a massive second period that proved the difference as they took a 1–0 lead after twenty minutes and turned it into a game-winning 3–0 lead. They added a goal early in the third, which forced Vancouver coach Alain Vigneault to pull goalie Roberto Luongo and give Cory Schneider his first taste of Stanley Cup Final play.

While the Bruins continued to be inspired by the injury to Nathan Horton, the Sedins continued to play on the periphery, unwilling to go hard to the net or play a physical game. The result was an ineffective offence that was stifled further by the flawless play of Tim Thomas in the Boston goal.

There were three lineup changes tonight. For Vancouver, Aaron Rome was out with his series-ending suspension, and in his place was Keith Ballard. As well, Jeff Tambellini was a healthy scratch and Tanner Glass was inserted for the first time in the Stanley Cup

Rich Peverley celebrates his first-period goal which got the Bruins off and running to victory.

Stanley Cup Final — Boston Bruins vs. Vancouver Canucks

83

Peverley beats Roberto Luongo by sliding the puck through the goalie's pads on a breakaway.

Final. And for Boston, rookie sensation Tyler Seguin was in the lineup to replace Horton.

The Bruins got the only goal of the first period thanks to a great play by David Krejci at the Vancouver blue-line. He dove to poke the puck free, and Rich Peverley went in alone on goal, beating Luongo with a goal through the pads at 11:59. That was all the Bruins needed to swing the momentum in their favour this night. Vancouver simply couldn't match the intensity or pace the Bruins came at their opponents with, and that slim lead never seemed in danger.

In the second, the two Boston goals came in a two-minute stretch in the middle part of the period. Michael Ryder took a routine shot from the top of the circle which may or may not have been tipped by defenceman Sami Salo, but it eluded Luongo even though the goalie should have had the shot.

Brad Marchand made it 3–0 on a great play from Patrice Bergeron. He went in behind the Vancouver net to get the puck, and Henrik Sedin wanted nothing to do with a bodycheck and moved out of the way, losing the puck and the angle to the goal at the same time. Bergeron got the puck out front and Marchand back-handed it over the big glove of Luongo.

Peverley added his second of the night at 3:39 of the third, and that was the game. Vancouver now had

to find a way to stem the incredible tide that was the Bruins' confidence, and it had to be prepared to "get dirty" in the tough areas of the ice if it were going to have any chance to use home ice to its advantage.

Said Thomas: "Every time this year that we've faced adversity as a team, we've rose to the challenge. We needed to do it one more time because we were down 2–0. Now we've done that for two games. The challenge for us will be to keep doing that."

The Bruins got a further lift when Horton, released from hospital only the previous day with a serious concussion, visited his teammates in the dressing room after the victory.

"I was very, very happy to see Nathan up and around in the locker room," Thomas said. "I wasn't exactly sure of his status."

"It's 2–2 and that's the way you look at it," said beleaguered Vancouver defenceman Kevin Bieksa. "They won their two at home and we won our two, so it looks like it could be a homer series and luckily we have two of the next three at home."

The Bruins faced two must-win games at home and won, and now Vancouver faced a must-win game. To lose game five would mean going to Boston with the Stanley Cup in the building and the Bruins ready to win.

84

Stanley Cup Final — Boston Bruins vs. Vancouver Canucks

Jubilant Bruins in front and disconsolate goalie Roberto Luongo in back. That was the story for game four.

Stanley Cup Final — Boston Bruins vs. Vancouver Canucks

85

GAME FIVE — *June 10, 2011*

Boston 0 at **Vancouver 1**
(Vancouver leads series 3-2)

After five games this series could now clearly be divided into two—Vancouver home games, all won by the home team with a dramatic and late goals, and Boston games which were two lop-sided victories, also by the home side. More particularly, it might be divided into games in which the goalies did, or didn't do, their thing.

Vancouver goalie Roberto Luongo was sensational at home, and he struggled on the road. More interestingly, Tim Thomas was incredible in all games, but in the three Vancouver wins he allowed a decisive goal in each as a result of his aggressive style of play. Tonight, Luongo stopped all 31 shots he faced, while Thomas was one shy of perfection, stopping 24 of 25.

Perhaps most frustrating for the Bruins, they were not able to carry their sensational play at home and take it to Rogers Arena. The momentum they had worked so hard to re-claim was lost again.

"It's the Stanley Cup Final, nobody said it was going to be easy," Lapierre said. "We just had to regroup and bounce back, and this is what we did. We were patient with the game plan, and we got our break."

In game five, the hero was Maxim Lapierre, who scored the only goal of the game at 4:35 of the third period on a sensational play. Kevin Bieksa had the puck at the right point and saw Thomas come well out to challenge him as he prepared to shoot. There was a scrum of players in front, but off to the back side was Lapierre. Bieksa, who must have played some snooker in his day, fired a shot off the end boards that came out the other side of the net right onto Lapierre's stick. He fired quickly, and Thomas dove back to snare the puck—but it had already crossed the goal line.

Defenceman Kevin Bieska watches as goalie Roberto Luongo makes a fine glove save.

86

Stanley Cup Final — Boston Bruins vs. Vancouver Canucks

Boston's Andrew Ference lets go a shot that Chris Higgins tries to block.

It was Vancouver's first goal in nearly 111 minutes of Cup Final play and came after Thomas had stoned Lapierre on a sure goal off the rush before the Canucks established possession in the Boston end.

"The way it was, it bounced off my stomach and was a couple inches over the line before I could get a handle on it," Thomas described.

Luongo unwisely stirred the pot when asked to comment about the goal. "It's not hard if you're playing in the paint," he said, comparing his more conservative style to Thomas's more gambling strategy. "It's an easy save for me, but if you're wandering out and aggressive like he does, that's going to happen."

Luongo could talk this night because that was all the scoring he needed. He played great down the stretch, including a huge left pad save off a Johnny Boychuk point shot through traffic with a couple of minutes left in the game.

Again, though, as had been the case all playoffs, the Bruins power play was a culprit on this night. Boston was given the first three power plays of the game yet couldn't cash in at a time when an early goal would have had a huge impact of the game.

"We knew right away early that we had some chances on the power play and we didn't do the job," Patrice Bergeron noted after his team went 0-for-4 with the man advantage. "It's plain and simple."

And now, the Canucks had a chance to take their energy, and Luongo's goaltending, and try to win the Stanley Cup. But they had to do it in inhospitable Boston.

"I don't think we're a team that's done anything the easy way," coach Claude Julien said. "We've been in two game sevens. Our goal right now is to create another one."

Stanley Cup Final — Boston Bruins vs. Vancouver Canucks

87

Too late. Boston goalie Tim Thomas reaches back to snare the puck, but it has already crossed the goal line for the only goal of the game.

GAME SIX — *June 13, 2011*

Vancouver 2 at **Boston** 5
(series tied 3-3)

Perhaps there has never been a stranger Stanley Cup Final series in NHL history. The Vancouver Canucks, who had played such a disciplined, team-oriented game in three meetings in Rogers Arena during their three victories, simply fell apart in each of their three visits to TD Garden in three lop-sided losses.

And Canucks goalie Roberto Luongo, virtually unbeatable at home, was nothing short of disastrous on the road. Again this night he was chased from the crease, surrendering three early goals in a 5–2 loss.

In all, the Bruins scored four times in 4:14 of the early part of the game and waltzed to an easy victory to force a decisive seventh game.

The outcome might have been different had Henrik Sedin converted a superb slapshot pass from Kevin Bieksa on the first shift. It came from the point, bounced off the end boards and out the other side, just like Maxim Lapierre's goal in game five. As it was, the puck hopped over Sedin's stick. Things got worse when Mason Raymond was rammed backwards into the boards by Johnny Boychuk and left the game with a vertebrae compression fracture and was gone for the series.

Soon after, the Boston barrage began.

Jannik Hansen hits the side of the net on this breakaway as goalie Tim Thomas outwaits him on the deke.

Stanley Cup Final — Boston Bruins vs. Vancouver Canucks

89

David Krejci buries a cross-crease pass from Mark Recchi on a five-on-three in the third period.

Brad Marchand got some open ice down the right side, and as he barrelled in on goal he roofed a shot over the glove of Luongo at 5:35 to open the scoring. Luongo was on his knees long before the shot left Marchand's stick. Just thirty-five seconds later, Milan Lucic knifed a shot that squirted between Luongo's pads and rolled over the goal line. Coach Alain Vigneault might have given his goalie the hook then because it was clear Luongo wasn't on his game, but he waited one more goal.

That came just two minutes later when an Andrew Ference point shot beat the goalie cleanly. Cory Schneider came in and was sensational the rest of the way, although the Bruins did make it 4–0 soon after when Michael Ryder tipped Tomas Kaberle's point shot off the post and in. Vigneault called a timeout, and although it had a calming effect, the damage had been done.

Vancouver might have gotten back in the game late in the first, but Jannik Hansen was only able to get off a weak shot on a breakaway. The Canucks continued to struggle on the power play in the series, failing to convert on two chances in the second and making it 0-for-20 in the series. They managed to get their first with the extra man just twenty-two seconds into the third, but that's as close as they got.

Henrik Sedin got that goal, moving into the slot, outwaiting Thomas, and roofing a backhand, but

Boston made in 5–1 during a five-on-three power play a few minutes later when David Krejci converted a great cross-crease pass from Mark Recchi.

Maxim Lapierre got a late goal for the Canucks to close out the scoring, and game seven was slated for two nights later. The Canucks had home ice, but the Bruins had the momentum. The outcome was undecided, but one thing was absolutely certain. The Cup would be in the building, and one team was going to skate off the ice with it.

"We've created ourselves another opportunity, and it's up to us to take advantage of it," said Boston coach Claude Julien. "But we've got to be hungrier than we have been the last three times in Vancouver."

The unflappable Luongo continued to exude confidence in the face of adversity. "I have to believe in myself, right? That's a big component of bouncing back and playing a good game," he suggested. "We're going to put what happened tonight behind us and get ready for what is going to be a dream as far as playing in game seven of the Stanley Cup Final."

Bruins players celebrate after their convincing 5-2 win to force a deciding game seven.

Stanley Cup Final — Boston Bruins vs. Vancouver Canucks

91

GAME SEVEN — *June 15, 2011*

Boston 4 at Vancouver 0

(Boston wins series 4–3)

Patrice Bergeron became just the twenty-fifth member of the Triple Gold Club, and he did so in style, scoring two goals in the first forty minutes to take the Boston Bruins to a 4–0 victory and the Stanley Cup. Brad Marchand also scored twice for the victors.

Most amazing, though, is that the Canucks, the highest scoring team in the regular season, scored just eight goals in seven games against the sensational Tim Thomas, named Conn Smythe Trophy winner after the game. The Bruins, meanwhile, counted twenty-three goals against an often shaky Roberto Luongo (who himself would have joined the TGC with a win).

The Boston Bruins were Stanley Cup champions for the first time in thirty-nine years. Interestingly, it was thirty-nine years between Cup wins in 1941 and 1970 as well.

Bergeron has now won the Stanley Cup, Olympic gold, and World Championship gold—the three requirements for Triple Gold Club membership.

It was the last game of the year and the Stanley Cup was in the building. So, too, were Mason Raymond of Vancouver and Nathan Horton of Boston, two players badly injured but making the trip to the Rogers Arena for the grand finale. Boston hadn't won the Cup since 1972. Vancouver hadn't ever won the Cup since joining the league in 1970. A Canadian team hadn't won the Cup since Montreal in 1993, but Canada did win Olympic gold in this

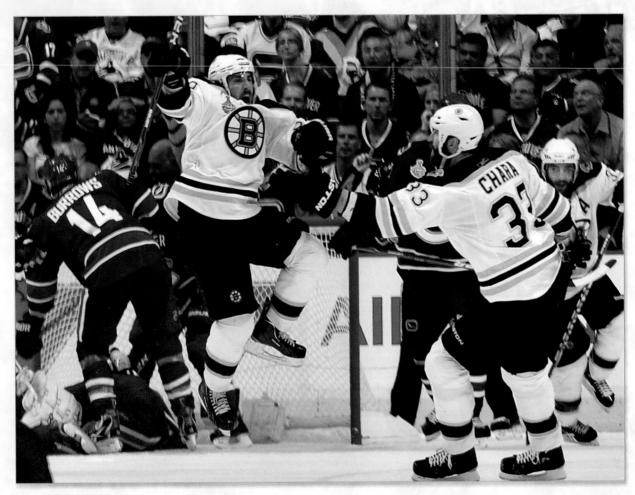

Boston's Brad Marchand leaps for joy after scoring on a wraparound to give the Bruins a 2–0 lead in the second period.

92

Stanley Cup Final — Boston Bruins vs. Vancouver Canucks

Bruins players begin a celebration that lasted all night after winning the Stanley Cup.

very building only sixteen months earlier—with Roberto Luongo in goal.

The home team had scored the first goal of every game so far and won all six games of the series so far. Both teams, looking nervous, had a couple of good chances early that they couldn't convert. For the Bruins, David Krejci threw the puck into the crease where Luongo managed to swipe it away. For Vancouver, Henrik Sedin and Chris Higgins had the puck in front but couldn't get it past Tim Thomas.

As it turned out, for the first time in the series, the visiting team scored the game's first goal, and it was a dandy. Brad Marchand got the puck deep in the Vancouver end off a faceoff won by the Canucks, and after cycling in the corner he spotted Bergeron in the slot. Marchand made a superb backhand pass through three Vancouver players, and Bergeron snapped a one-timer off the far post and past a stunned Luongo at 14:37.

The goal silenced the crowd, but Ryan Kesler came back moments later with a great chance. Thomas again had perfect body position and made a tough save look easy. The period ended 1–0 for the Bruins, Boston scoring in the opening period of a road game for the first time in the four games of this series.

Boston played a sensational road period in the second, getting the puck deep and forechecking aggressively, making it tough for the Canucks even to get out of their own end. Vancouver had no luck on the slow ice as pucks bounced over their sticks at the worst times, and the Bruins capitalized on their few scoring chances.

In the second, two more errors by Luongo sealed Vancouver's fate. He mishandled a routine point shot, and Marchand got the puck to one side of the net and wrapped it into the far side. Luongo had made the save, but his momentum carried the puck over the goal line.

Then, late in the period, Bergeron stole the puck at his blue-line with the Canucks on a power play. He tore down the ice, being chased by Sami Salo, who was going to get a penalty, but Bergeron got a shot off, fell into the net, and took the puck with him as Luongo gave up on the play. That 3–0 goal at 17:35 was the fatal blow. Everyone knew Thomas was not about to surrender three goals in the final twenty minutes. Indeed, everyone knew he would be named Conn Smythe Trophy winner if the Bruins won the Cup (and perhaps even if they didn't).

The third period was all about shutting down the Canucks, which the Bruins did to perfection. Marchand got his second into an empty net as coach Alain Vigneault did what he could to get his team on the board. After the final horn, the Bruins poured onto the ice and celebrated a remarkable victory at the end of a rigourous and spectacular season.

Stanley Cup Final — Boston Bruins vs. Vancouver Canucks

93

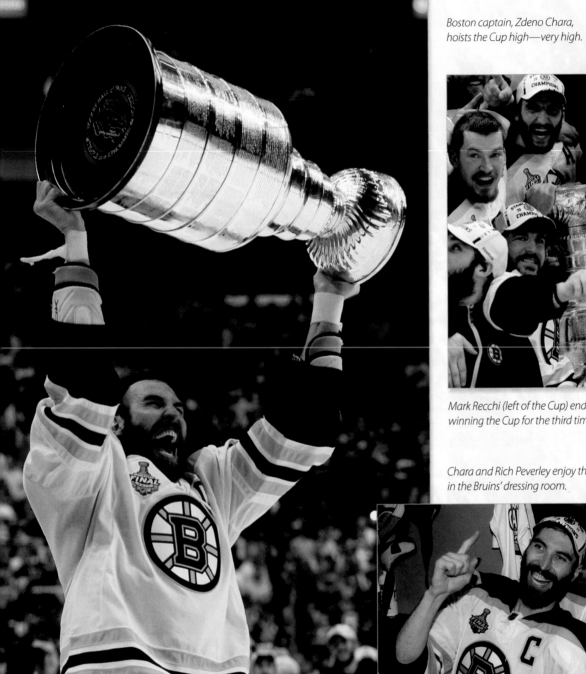

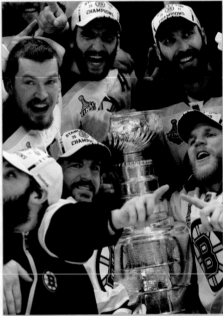

Boston captain, Zdeno Chara, hoists the Cup high—very high.

Mark Recchi (left of the Cup) ended his career by winning the Cup for the third time.

Chara and Rich Peverley enjoy the celebrations in the Bruins' dressing room.

Goalie Tim Thomas was easily the best player in the post-season and won the Conn Smythe Trophy as a result.

Johnny Boychuk confirms it's love—with Lord Stanley's bowl—sealing the deal with a kiss.

The elated and exhausted Bruins enjoy their Cup moments on ice.

Stanley Cup Final — Boston Bruins vs. Vancouver Canucks

95

The Boston Bruins won their first Stanley Cup in 1928–29, only their fifth year in the NHL. The team's rise had been meteoric thanks largely to the wiles of general manager and coach, Art Ross. In the team's first year, it finished dead last of six teams. A year later, it was fourth of seven, and in 1926–27, the league expanded to ten teams which now split into two divisions, Canadian and American (though not all teams in the Canadian Division were located in Canada).

In 1926–27, the Bruins finished second in the American Division, well back of the Rangers, and a year later the teams flipped positions. The Rangers won the Cup in 1928, but in 1928–29 the Bruins again finished on top of the division with an impressive 26–13–5 record for the forty-four-game schedule. They led all teams in wins with twenty-six and were second in goals against, allowing only fifty-two (the Montreal Canadiens allowed forty-three).

In the playoffs, the Bruins were perfect. They swept the Canadiens in three straight games of their best-of-five, advancing to the Cup final, and then they beat the Rangers in two straight of their best-of-three final. This marked the first time two U.S. teams competed for the Cup.

The team's roster was a who's who of great players of the era. Leading the way was defenceman Eddie Shore and forwards Dit Clapper and Cooney Weiland. Mickey MacKay and Cy Denneny were on the team, and rookie goalie Tiny Thompson played every minute of every game for the team this year. Ross, of course, was still in charge. All of these men were later inducted into the Hockey Hall of Fame. To have six such stars on a roster of sixteen is incredible, to say the least.

Eddie Shore was the first great superstar signed by the Bruins and the main reason the team won the Stanley Cup in 1929.

While the roster of the Bruins teams that won the Stanley Cup twice in three years during the early days of the war was radically different from the initial 1929 team, there were some shared attributes. Art Ross, for instance, continued to be the general manager and coach; the guiding force of the team.

Two youngsters in 1929, Cooney Weiland and Dit Clapper, were now veterans who captained the 1939 and 1941 team, respectively, to victory. Eddie Shore was there in 1939 towards the end of his sensational career. But what these teams had that 1929 didn't have was the Kraut Line—Woody Dumart, Bobby Bauer, Milt Schmidt.

Theirs was a great story. Born in Kitchener, Ontario (which had been renamed from Berlin in 1916 just before their births), the three were childhood friends who played hockey and developed together. They joined the Bruins at pretty much the same time, were put on a line together, and flourished for years as one of the top-scoring lines in the game. As a result of their hometown, the three became known as the Kraut Line.

Starting in 1938–39, the NHL reverted from two divisions to one, and the Bruins finished in first place for three straight years, through to 1941–42. In 1939–40, the three Kraut Line players finished 1–2–3 in league scoring, the first time three members of the same team finished in the top three positions. Ironically, this was the only year of the three that the Bruins didn't win the Stanley Cup.

In 1938–39, the Bruins had a 36–10–2 record, and their 74 points was miles ahead of second place Rangers (58). In the playoffs, things weren't so one-sided. In the first round, the top two teams met, and the Bruins needed a goal from Mel Hill in the third overtime to eliminate the Rangers. It was Hill's third OT winner of the series, a feat never accomplished before or since. It was also the first time that the NHL adopted best-of-seven series to decide playoff winners.

That win advanced the Bruins to the Stanley Cup Final where they had an easier time, defeating the Leafs in five games to win their second Cup. In 1939–40, the Rangers took care of Boston in six games as the top two teams met again in the opening round.

In 1940–41, the Bruins lost only eight of forty-eight games. They beat the Leafs in seven games in the first round of the playoffs, and in the final they swamped Detroit in four straight games. In goal for both Cup wins was another Hall of Famer, Frank Brimsek, who played every game for the Bruins that season. These were to be the last wins for the Bruins for nearly three decades.

The Kraut Line featured (l-r) Milt Schmidt, Woody Dumart, and Bobby Bauer and was key to the Bruins' Cup victories in 1939 and 1941.

The hockey world had changed to such a degree between 1941 and 1970 that there was little recognizable between the eras. In 1969–70, when the Bruins won the Cup for the first time in twenty-nine years, there were twelve teams, not seven. The players flew to games by plane rather than take trains. They went as far west as California, and now played seventy-six games a season, not forty-eight.

And in the modern era, the Bruins had Bobby Orr and Phil Esposito, and the team's goalie, Gerry Cheevers, wore a mask, an inconceivable piece of equipment in the days of Frank Brimsek.

But the key to victory was number four, Bobby Orr. The young defenceman was in his fourth NHL season, the most dominant player of his generation, whose spectacular skating made him a fearless sensation from the blue-line. In this year, he won the Art Ross Trophy by accumulating 120 points, the only defenceman ever to win the scoring race. He beat out Esposito by a whopping twenty-one points and was, in fact, the only NHLer to pass 100 points this season. His goal scoring was unmatched for a defenceman, and his passing sensational. It was much like having a fourth forward on the ice whenever he played—and he played a lot.

The Bruins beat the Rangers in six games in the opening round of the playoffs, and then swept Chicago in four straight, outscoring the Hawks 20–10. In the Stanley Cup Final, the Bruins played the St. Louis Blues. In the first few years after the major expansion from six to twelve teams in 1967, the Original Six teams were put in one division and the expansion teams in the other. This allowed for a Stanley Cup Final to feature an old and a new team, so although the results were never close, it gave the new teams a chance to grow the game in their cities.

In 1970, the Bruins won the first three games easily, defeating the Blues 6–1, 6–2, and 4–1. But game four went to overtime as teams were tied 3–3 after regulation. Just forty seconds into the OT, Orr took a pass from Derek Sanderson, beat Glenn Hall with a quick shot, and was hooked at the ankle by Noel Picard, resulting in his flying through the air in celebration. It might not have ended the greatest series ever, but it was surely the most memorable Cup-winning photograph ever shot (rivaled only by Bill Barilko's 1951 Cup winner by the Leafs over Montreal, all five games of which went to overtime and which was also made famous by several memorable photos).

The Bruins repeated as Cup champs in 1972. They finished first overall in the standings and then tore through the playoffs, beating Toronto in five games, sweeping the Blues again, and finally meeting some opposition in the Final, downing the Rangers in six games. These were the only two Cup wins for Orr, Esposito, Cheevers, and their great teammates, but these teams were as great as any that ever won the Stanley Cup. The Bruins were tough as nails, scored at a record pace, and played exciting hockey every minute of every game.

Bobby Orr flies through the air after scoring the winning goal against St. Louis's Glenn Hall in game four of the 1970 Stanley Cup Final.

	GP	W	L	T/OT	GF	GA	Pts
1924-25	30	6	24	0	42	119	12
1925-26	36	17	15	4	92	85	38
1926-27	44	21	20	3	97	89	45
1927-28	44	20	13	11	77	70	51
1928-29	44	26	13	5	89	52	57
1929-30	44	38	5	1	179	98	77
1930-31	44	28	10	6	143	90	62
1931-32	48	15	21	12	122	117	42
1932-33	48	25	15	8	124	88	58
1933-34	48	18	25	5	111	130	41
1934-35	48	26	16	6	129	112	58
1935-36	48	22	20	6	92	83	50
1936-37	48	23	18	7	120	110	53
1937-38	48	30	11	7	142	89	67
1938-39	48	36	10	2	156	76	74
1939-40	48	31	12	5	170	98	67
1940-41	48	27	8	13	168	102	67
1941-42	48	25	17	6	160	118	56
1942-43	50	24	17	9	195	176	57
1943-44	50	19	26	5	223	268	43
1944-45	50	16	30	4	179	219	36
1945-46	50	24	18	8	167	156	56
1946-47	60	26	23	11	190	175	63
1947-48	60	23	24	13	178	168	59
1948-49	60	29	23	8	198	163	66
1949-50	70	22	32	16	178	228	60
1950-51	70	22	30	18	162	197	62
1951-52	70	25	29	16	162	176	66
1952-53	70	28	29	13	152	172	69
1953-54	70	32	28	10	177	181	74
1954-55	70	23	26	21	169	188	67
1955-56	70	23	34	13	147	185	59
1956-57	70	34	24	12	195	174	80
1957-58	70	27	28	5	199	194	69
1958-59	70	32	29	9	205	215	73
1959-60	70	28	34	8	220	241	64
1960-61	70	15	42	13	176	254	43
1961-62	70	15	47	8	177	306	38
1962-63	70	14	39	17	198	281	45
1963-64	70	18	40	12	170	212	48
1964-65	70	21	43	6	166	253	48
1965-66	70	21	43	6	174	275	48
1966-67	70	17	43	10	182	253	44
1967-68	74	37	27	10	259	216	84
1968-69	76	42	18	16	303	221	100
1969-70	76	40	17	19	277	216	99
1970-71	78	57	14	7	399	207	121
1971-72	78	54	13	11	330	204	119
1972-73	78	51	22	5	330	235	107
1973-74	78	52	17	9	349	221	113
1974-75	80	40	26	14	345	245	94
1975-76	80	49	15	17	313	237	113
1976-77	80	49	23	8	312	240	106
1977-78	80	51	18	11	333	218	113
1978-79	80	43	23	14	316	270	100
1979-80	80	46	21	13	310	234	105
1980-81	80	37	30	13	316	272	87
1981-82	80	43	27	10	323	285	96
1982-83	80	50	20	10	327	228	110
1983-84	80	49	25	6	336	261	104
1984-85	80	36	34	10	303	287	82
1985-86	80	37	31	12	311	288	86
1986-87	80	39	34	7	301	276	85
1987-88	80	44	30	6	300	251	94
1988-89	80	37	29	14	289	256	88
1989-90	80	46	25	9	289	232	101
1990-91	80	44	24	12	299	264	100
1991-92	80	36	32	12	270	275	84
1992-93	84	51	26	7	332	268	109
1993-94	84	42	29	13	289	252	97
1994-95	48	27	18	3	150	127	57
1995-96	82	40	31	11	282	269	91
1996-97	82	26	47	9	234	300	61
1997-98	82	39	30	13	221	194	91
1998-99	82	39	30	13	214	181	91
1999-2000	82	24	33	19	210	248	73
2000-01	82	36	30	8	227	249	88
2001-02	82	43	24	6	236	201	101
2002-03	82	36	31	11	245	237	87
2003-04	82	41	19	15	209	188	104
2004-05		NO SEASON					
2005-06	82	29	37	16	230	266	74
2006-07	82	35	41	6	219	289	76
2007-08	82	41	29	12	212	222	94
2008-09	82	53	19	10	274	196	116
2009-10	82	39	30	13	206	200	91
2010-11	82	46	25	11	246	195	103

PREVIOUS PLAYOFF RESULTS

2009-10

Beat Buffalo, 4-2, in Eastern Conference quarter-final
Lost to Philadelphia, 4-3, in Eastern Conference semi-final

2008-09

Beat Montreal, 4-0, in Eastern Conference quarter-final
Lost to Carolina, 4-3, in Eastern Conference semi-final

2007-08

Lost to Montreal, 4-3, in Eastern Conference quarter-final

2006-07　　　DNQ

2005-06　　　DNQ

2004-05　　　NO SEASON

2003-04

Lost to Montreal, 4-3, in Eastern Conference quarter-final

2002-03

Lost to New Jersey, 4-1, in Eastern Conference quarter-final

2001-02

Lost to Montreal, 4-2, in Eastern Conference quarter-final

2000-01 DNQ

1999-2000　　　DNQ

1998-99

Beat Carolina, 4-2, in Eastern Conference quarter-final
Lost to Buffalo, 4-2, in Eastern Conference semi-final

1997-98

Lost to Washington, 4-2, in Eastern Conference quarter-final

1996-97　　　DNQ

1995-96

Lost to Florida, 4-1, in Eastern Conference quarter-final

1994-95

Lost to New Jersey, 4-1, in Eastern Conference quarter-final

1993-94

Beat Montreal, 4-3, in Eastern Conference quarter-final
Lost to New Jersey, 4-2, in Eastern Conference semi-final

1992-93

Lost to Buffalo, 4-0, in Adams Division semi-final

1991-92

Beat Buffalo, 4-3, in Adams Division semi-final
Beat Montreal, 4-0, in Adams Division final
Lost to Pittsburgh, 4-0, in Wales Conference final

1990-91

Beat Hartford, 4-2, in Adams Division semi-final
Beat Montreal, 4-3, in Adams Division final
Lost to Pittsburgh, 4-2, in Wales Conference final

1989-90

Beat Hartford, 4-3, in Adams Division semi-final
Beat Montreal, 4-1, in Adams Division final
Beat Washington, 4-0, in Wales Conference final
Lost to Edmonton, 4-1, in Stanley Cup Final

1988-89

Beat Buffalo, 4-1, in Adams Division semi-final
Lost to Montreal, 4-1, in Adams Division final

1987-88

Beat Buffalo, 4-2, in Adams Division semi-final
Beat Montreal, 4-1, in Adams Division final
Beat New Jersey, 4-3, in Wales Conference final
Lost to Edmonton, 4-0, Stanley Cup Final

1986-87

Lost to Montreal, 4-0, in Adams Division semi-final

1985-86

Lost to Montreal, 3-0, in Adams Division semi-final

1984-85

Lost to Montreal, 3-2, in Adams Division semi-final

1983-84

Lost to Montreal, 3-0, in Adams Division semi-final

1982-83

Beat Quebec, 3-1, in Adams Division semi-final
Beat Buffalo, 4-3, in Adams Division final
Lost to NY Islanders, 4-2, in Wales Conference final

1981-82

Beat Buffalo, 3-1, in Adams Division semi-final
Lost to Quebec, 4-3, in Adams Division final

1980-81

Lost to Minnesota, 3-0, in preliminary round

1979-80

Beat Pittsburgh, 3-2, in preliminary round
Lost to NY Islanders, 4-2, in quarter-final

1978-79

Beat Pittsburgh, 4-0, in quarter-final
Lost to Montreal, 4-3, in semi-final

1977-78

Beat Chicago, 4-0, in quarter-final
Beat Philadelphia, 4-1, in semi-final
Lost to Montreal, 4-2, in Stanley Cup Final

1976-77

Beat Los Angeles, 4-2, in quarter-final
Beat Philadelphia, 4-0, in semi-final
Lost to Montreal, 4-0, in Stanley Cup Final

1975-76

Beat Los Angeles, 4-3, in quarter-final
Lost to Philadelphia, 4-1, in semi-final

1974-75

Lost to Chicago, 2-1, in preliminary round

1973-74

Beat Toronto, 4-0, in quarter-final
Beat Chicago, 4-2, in semi-final
Lost to Philadelphia, 4-2, in Stanley Cup Final

1972-73

Lost to NY Rangers, 4-1, in quarter-final

1971-72

Beat Toronto, 4-1, in quarter-final
Beat St. Louis, 4-0, in semi-final
Beat NY Rangers, 4-2, in Stanley Cup Final

1970-71

Lost to Montreal, 4-3, in quarter-final

1969-70

Beat NY Rangers, 4-2, in quarter-final
Beat Chicago, 4-0, in semi-final
Beat St. Louis, 4-0, in Stanley Cup Final

1968-69

Beat Toronto, 4-0, in quarter-final
Lost to Montreal, 4-2, in semi-final

1967-68

Lost to Montreal, 4-0, in quarter-final

1966-67   DNQ

1965-66   DNQ

1964-65   DNQ

1963-64   DNQ

1962-63   DNQ

1961-62   DNQ

1960-61   DNQ

1959-60   DNQ

1958-59

Lost to Toronto, 4-3, in semi-final

1957-58

Beat NY Rangers, 4-2, in semi-final
Lost to Montreal, 4-2, in Stanley Cup Final

1956-57

Beat Detroit, 4-1, in semi-final
Lost to Montreal, 4-1, in Stanley Cup Final

1955-56 DNQ

1954-55

Lost to Montreal, 4-1, in semi-final

1953-54

Lost to Montreal, 4-0, in semi-final

1952-53

Beat Detroit, 4-2, in semi-final
Lost to Montreal, 4-1, in Stanley Cup Final

1951-52

Lost to Montreal, 4-3, in semi-final

1950-51

Lost to Toronto, 4-1, in semi-final

1949-50   DNQ

1948-49

Lost to Toronto, 4-1, in semi-final

1947-48

Lost to Toronto, 4-1, in semi-final

1946-47

Lost to Montreal, 4-1, in semi-final

1945-46

Beat Detroit, 4-1 in semi-final
Lost to Montreal, 4-1, in Stanley Cup Final

1944-45

Lost to Detroit, 4-3, in semi-final

1943-44   DNQ

1942-43

Beat Montreal, 4-1, in semi-final
Lost to Detroit, 4-0, in Stanley Cup Final

1941-42

Lost to Detroit, 2-0, in quarter-final

1940-41

Beat Toronto, 4-3, in semi-final
Beat Detroit, 4-0, in Stanley Cup Final

1939-40

Lost to NY Rangers, 4-2, in semi-final

1938-39

Beat NY Rangers, 4-3, in semi-final
Beat Toronto, 4-1, in Stanley Cup Final

1937-38

Lost to Toronto, 3-0, in semi-final

1936-37

Lost to Montreal Maroons, 2-1, in quarter-final

1935-36

Lost to Toronto, 8-6, in total goals quarter-final

1934-35

Lost to Toronto, 3-1, in semi-final

1933-34   DNQ

1932-33

Lost to Toronto, 3-2, in semi-final

1931-32   DNQ

1930-31

Lost to Montreal, 3-2, in semi-final

1929-30

Beat Montreal Maroons, 3-1, in semi-final
Lost to Montreal, 2-0, in Stanley Cup Final

1928-29

Beat Montreal, 3-0, in semi-final
Beat NY Rangers, 2-0, in Stanley Cup Final

1927-28

Lost to NY Rangers, 5-2, in total goals quarter-final

1926-27

Beat Chicago, 10-5, in total goals quarter-final
Beat NY Rangers, 3-1, in total goals semi-final
Lost to Ottawa, 7-3, in total goals Stanley Cup Final

1925-26   DNQ

1924-25   DNQ

Year	Team	Position	Player
1930-31	Second	Right Wing	**Dit Clapper**
1930-31	Second	Goal	**Tiny Thompson**
1931-32	First	Defence	**Eddie Shore**
1932-33	First	Defence	**Eddie Shore**
1933-34	Second	Defence	**Eddie Shore**
1934-35	First	Defence	**Eddie Shore**
1934-35	Second	Goal	**Tiny Thompson**
1934-35	Second	Right Wing	**Dit Clapper**
1935-36	First	Defence	**Eddie Shore**
1935-36	First	Goal	**Tiny Thompson**
1935-36	First	Defence	**Babe Siebert**
1937-38	First	Defence	**Eddie Shore**
1937-38	First	Goal	**Tiny Thompson**
1937-38	First	Centre	**Bill Cowley**
1937-38	Second	Coach	**Art Ross**
1938-39	First	Defence	**Eddie Shore**
1938-39	First	Goal	**Frank Brimsek**
1938-39	First	Defence	**Dit Clapper**
1938-39	First	Coach	**Art Ross**
1938-39	Second	Right Wing	**Bobby Bauer**
1939-40	First	Defence	**Dit Clapper**
1939-40	First	Centre	**Milt Schmidt**
1939-40	Second	Goal	**Frank Brimsek**
1939-40	Second	Right Wing	**Bobby Bauer**
1939-40	Second	Left Wing	**Woody Dumart**
1940-41	First	Defence	**Dit Clapper**
1940-41	First	Centre	**Bill Cowley**
1940-41	First	Coach	**Cooney Weiland**
1940-41	Second	Goal	**Frank Brimsek**
1940-41	Second	Right Wing	**Bobby Bauer**
1940-41	Second	Left Wing	**Woody Dumart**
1941-42	First	Goal	**Frank Brimsek**
1942-43	First	Centre	**Bill Cowley**
1942-43	Second	Goal	**Frank Brimsek**
1942-43	Second	Defence	**Jack Crawford**
1942-43	Second	Defence	**Flash Hollett**
1942-43	Second	Coach	**Art Ross**
1943-44	First	Centre	**Bill Cowley**
1943-44	Second	Defence	**Dit Clapper**
1943-44	Second	Left Wing	**Herb Cain**
1944-45	Second	Centre	**Bill Cowley**
1945-46	First	Defence	**Jack Crawford**
1945-46	Second	Goal	**Frank Brimsek**
1946-47	First	Centre	**Milt Schmidt**
1946-47	Second	Goal	**Frank Brimsek**
1946-47	Second	Left Wing	**Woody Dumart**
1947-48	Second	Goal	**Frank Brimsek**
1950-51	First	Defence	**Bill Quackenbush**
1950-51	First	Centre	**Milt Schmidt**
1951-52	Second	Goal	**Jim Henry**
1951-52	Second	Centre	**Milt Schmidt**
1952-53	First	Centre	**Fleming Mackell**
1952-53	Second	Defence	**Bill Quackenbush**
1953-54	Second	Left Wing	**Ed Sandford**
1954-55	Second	Defence	**Fern Flaman**
1956-57	Second	Left Wing	**Real Chevrefils**
1957-58	Second	Defence	**Fern Flaman**
1959-60	Second	Centre	**Bronco Horvath**
1966-67	Second	Defence	**Bobby Orr**

1967-68	First	Defence	**Bobby Orr**
1968-68	Second	Centre	**Phil Esposito**
1967-68	Second	Left Wing	**Johnny Bucyk**
1968-69	First	Defence	**Bobby Orr**
1968-69	First	Centre	**Phil Esposito**
1968-69	Second	Defence	**Ted Green**
1969-70	First	Defence	**Bobby Orr**
1969-70	First	Centre	**Phil Esposito**
1969-70	Second	Right Wing	**John McKenzie**
1970-71	First	Defence	**Bobby Orr**
1970-71	First	Centre	**Phil Esposito**
1970-71	First	Right Wing	**Ken Hodge**
1970-71	First	Left Wing	**Johnny Bucyk**
1971-72	First	Defence	**Bobby Orr**
1971-72	First	Centre	**Phil Esposito**
1972-73	First	Defence	**Bobby Orr**
1972-73	First	Centre	**Phil Esposito**
1973-74	First	Defence	**Bobby Orr**
1973-74	First	Centre	**Phil Esposito**
1973-74	First	Right Wing	**Ken Hodge**
1973-74	Second	Left Wing	**Wayne Cashman**
1974-75	First	Defence	**Bobby Orr**
1974-75	Second	Centre	**Phil Esposito**
1975-76	First	Defence	**Brad Park**
1977-78	First	Defence	**Brad Park**
1979-80	First	Defence	**Ray Bourque**
1980-81	Second	Defence	**Ray Bourque**
1981-82	First	Defence	**Ray Bourque**
1981-82	Second	Right Wing	**Rick Middleton**
1982-83	Second	Defence	**Ray Bourque**
1982-83	First	Goal	**Pete Peeters**
1983-84	First	Defence	**Ray Bourque**
1984-85	First	Defence	**Ray Bourque**
1985-86	Second	Defence	**Ray Bourque**
1986-87	First	Defence	**Ray Bourque**
1987-88	First	Defence	**Ray Bourque**
1987-88	Second	Right Wing	**Cam Neely**
1988-89	Second	Defence	**Ray Bourque**
1989-90	First	Defence	**Ray Bourque**
1989-90	Second	Right Wing	**Cam Neely**
1990-91	First	Defence	**Ray Bourque**
1990-91	Second	Right Wing	**Cam Neely**
1991-92	First	Defence	**Ray Bourque**
1992-93	First	Defence	**Ray Bourque**
1993-94	First	Defence	**Ray Bourque**
1993-94	Second	Right Wing	**Cam Neely**
1994-95	Second	Defence	**Ray Bourque**
1995-96	First	Defence	**Ray Bourque**
1998-99	Second	Defence	**Ray Bourque**
2001-02	Second	Right Wing	**Bill Guerin**
2002-03	Second	Centre	**Joe Thornton**
2005-06	First	Centre	**Joe Thornton** *(also San Jose)*
2007-08	Second	Defence	**Zdeno Chara**
2008-09	First	Goal	**Tim Thomas**
2008-09	First	Defence	**Zdeno Chara**

BOSTON BRUINS IN THE HOCKEY HALL OF FAME

Charles Adams	(Builder, 1960)	Duke Keats	(Player, 1958)
Weston Adams	(Builder, 1972)	Guy Lapointe	(Player, 1993)
Marty Barry	(Player, 1965)	Harry Lumley	(Player, 1980)
Bobby Bauer	(Player, 1996)	Mickey MacKay	(Player, 1952)
Leo Boivin	(Player, 1986)	Sylvio Mantha	(Player, 1960)
Ray Bourque	(Player, 2004)	Joe Mullen	(Player, 2000)
Frank Brimsek	(Player, 1966)	Harry Oliver	(Player, 1967)
George Brown	(Builder, 1961)	Bobby Orr	(Player, 1979)
Walter A. Brown	(Builder, 1962)	Bernie Parent	(Player, 1984)
Johnny Bucyk	(Player, 1981)	Brad Park	(Player, (1988)
Billy Burch	(Player, 1974)	Jacques Plante	(Player, 1978)
Gerry Cheevers	(Player, 1985)	Babe Pratt	(Player, 1966)
Dit Clapper	(Player, 1947)	Bill Quackenbush	(Player, 1976)
Sprague Cleghorn	(Player, 1958)	Jean Ratelle	(Player, 1985)
Paul Coffey	(Player, 2004)	Art Ross	(Player, 1949)
Roy Conacher	(Player, 1998)	Terry Sawchuk	(Player, 1971)
Fred Cook	(Player, 1995)	Milt Schmidt	(Player, 1961)
Bill Cowley	(Player, 1968)	Eddie Shore	(Player, 1947)
Cy Denneny	(Player, 1959)	Babe Siebert	(Player, 1964)
Woody Dumart	(Player, 1992)	Harry Sinden	(Builder, 1983)
Phil Esposito	(Player, 1984)	Hooley Smith	(Player, 1972)
Fern Flaman	(Player, 1990)	Allan Stanley	(Player, 1981)
Frank Frederickson	(Player, 1958)	Nels Stewart	(Player, 1952)
Busher Jackson	(Player, 1971)	Tiny Thompson	(Player, 1959)
Tom Johnson	(Player, 1970)	Cooney Weiland	(Player, 1971)

Milt Schmidt's number 15 is raised to the rafters to join the distinguished few sweater numbers retired by the Bruins.

2   **Eddie Shore** (January 1, 1947)

3   **Lionel Hitchman** (February 22, 1934)

4   **Bobby Orr** (January 9, 1979)

5   **Dit Clapper** (February 12, 1947)

7   **Phil Esposito** (December 3, 1987)

8   **Cam Neely** (January 12, 2004)

9   **Johnny Bucyk** (March 13, 1980)

15   **Milt Schmidt** (March 13, 1980)

24   **Terry O'Reilly** (October 24, 2002)

77   **Ray Bourque** (October 4, 2001)

BOSTON BRUINS TROPHY WINNERS

Art Ross Trophy

1929-30	Cooney Weiland
1939-40	Milt Schmidt
1940-41	Bill Cowley
1943-44	Herb Cain
1968-69	Phil Esposito
1969-70	Bobby Orr
1970-71	Phil Esposito
1971-72	Phil Esposito
1972-73	Phil Esposito
1973-74	Phil Esposito
1974-75	Bobby Orr
2005-06	Joe Thornton
	(also San Jose)

Hart Trophy

1932-33	Eddie Shore
1934-35	Eddie Shore
1935-36	Eddie Shore
1937-38	Eddie Shore
1940-41	Bill Cowley
1942-43	Bill Cowley
1950-51	Milt Schmidt
1968-69	Phil Esposito
1969-70	Bobby Orr
1970-71	Bobby Orr
1971-72	Bobby Orr
1973-74	Phil Esposito
2005-06	Joe Thornton
	(also San Jose)

Lester B. Pearson Award

1970-71	Phil Esposito
1973-74	Phil Esposito
1974-75	Bobby Orr

James Norris Trophy

1967-68	Bobby Orr
1968-69	Bobby Orr
1969-70	Bobby Orr
1970-71	Bobby Orr
1971-72	Bobby Orr
1972-73	Bobby Orr
1973-74	Bobby Orr
1974-75	Bobby Orr
1986-87	Ray Bourque
1987-88	Ray Bourque
1989-90	Ray Bourque
1990-91	Ray Bourque
1993-94	Ray Bourque
2008-09	Zdeno Chara

Calder Trophy

1938-39	Frank Brimsek
1949-50	Jack Gelineau
1956-57	Larry Regan
1966-67	Bobby Orr
1967-68	Derek Sanderson
1979-80	Ray Bourque
1997-98	Sergei Samsonov
2003-04	Andrew Raycroft

Vezina Trophy

1929-30	Tiny Thompson
1932-33	Tiny Thompson
1935-36	Tiny Thompson
1937-38	Tiny Thompson
1938-39	Frank Brimsek
1941-42	Frank Brimsek
1982-83	Pete Peeters
2008-09	Tim Thomas

William Jennings Trophy

1989-90	Andy Moog/ Reggie Lemelin
2008-09	Tim Thomas/ Manny Fernandez

Lady Byng Trophy

1939-40	Bobby Bauer
1940-41	Bobby Bauer
1946-47	Bobby Bauer
1970-71	Johnny Bucyk
1973-74	Johnny Bucyk
1981-82	Rick Middleton

Conn Smythe Trophy

1970	Bobby Orr
1972	Bobby Orr

Bill Masterton Trophy

1985-86	Charlie Simmer
1989-90	Gord Kluzak
1993-94	Cam Neely
2006-07	Phil Kessel

Frank Selke Trophy

1981-82	Steve Kasper

King Clancy Trophy

1991-92	Ray Bourque
1992-93	Dave Poulin

Jack Adams Award

1975-76	Don Cherry
1997-98	Pat Burns
2008-09	Claude Julien

BOSTON BRUINS DRAFT CHOICES, 1963-2010

1963

3	Orest Romashyna
9	Terrance Lane
14	Roger Bamburak
19	Jim Blair

1964

2	Alex Campbell
8	Jim Booth
14	Ken Dryden
20	Blair Allister

1965

4	Joe Bailey
9	Bill Ramsay

1966

1	Barry Gibbs
7	Rick Smith
13	Garnet "Ace" Bailey
19	Tom Webster

1967

10	Meehan Bonnar

1968

12	Danny Schock
18	Fraser Rice
24	Brian St. John

1969

3	Don Tannahill
4	Frank Spring
11	Ivan Boldirev
22	Art Quoquochi
34	Nels Jacobson
46	Ron Fairbrother
58	Jeremy Wright
69	Jim Jones

1970

3	Reggie Leach
4	Rick MacLeish
9	Ron Plumb
13	Bob Stewart
27	Dan Bouchard
41	Ray Brownlee
55	Gord Davies
69	Bob Roselle
83	Murray Wing
96	Glenn Siddall

1971

6	Ron Jones
14	Terry O'Reilly
28	Curt Ridley
42	Dave Bonter
56	Dave Hynes
70	Bert Scott
84	Bob McMahon

1972

16	Mike Bloom
32	Wayne Elder
48	Michel Boudreau
64	Les Jackson
80	Brian Coates
96	Peter Gaw
112	Gordie Clark
128	Roy Carmichael

1973

6	Andre Savard
31	Jimmy Jones
36	Doug Gibson
47	Al Sims
63	Steve Langdon
79	Peter Crosbie
95	Jean-Pierre Bourgouyne
111	Walter Johnson
127	Virgil Gates
142	Jim Pettie
157	Yvon Bouillon

1974

18	Don Larway
25	Mark Howe
36	Peter Sturgeon
54	Tom Edur
72	Bill Reed
90	Jamie Bateman
108	Bill Best
126	Ray Maluta
143	Daryl Drader
160	Peter Roberts
175	Peter Waselovich

1975

14	Doug Halward
32	Barry Smith
60	Rick Adduono
68	Denis Daigle
86	Stan Jonathan
104	Matti Hagman
122	Gary Carr
140	Bo Berglund
156	Joe Rando
171	Kevin Nugent

1976

16	Clayton Pachal
34	Lorry Gloeckner
70	Bob Miller
88	Pete Vandemark
106	Ted Olson

1977

16	Dwight Foster
34	Dave Parro
52	Mike Forbes
70	Brian McGregor
88	Doug Butler
106	Keith Johnson
122	Ralph Cox
138	Mario Claude

1978

16	Al Secord
35	Graeme Nicolson
52	Brad Knelson
68	George Buat
85	Darryl McLeod
102	Jeff Brubaker
119	Murray Skinner
136	Bobby Hehir
153	Craig MacTavish

1979

8	Ray Bourque
15	Brad McCrimmon
36	Doug Morrison
57	Keith Crowder
78	Larry Melnyk
99	Marco Baron
120	Mike Krushelnyski

1980

18	Barry Pederson
60	Tom Fergus
81	Steve Kasper
102	Randy Hillier
123	Steve Lyons
144	Anthony McMurchy
165	Mike Moffat
186	Michael Thelven
207	Jens Ohling

1981

14	Normand Leveille
35	Luc Dufour
77	Scott McLellan
98	Joe Mantione
119	Bruce Milton
140	Mats Thelin
161	Armel Parisee
182	Don Sylvestri
203	Richard Bourque

1982

1	Gord Kluzak
22	Brian Curran
39	Lyndon Byers
60	Dave Reid
102	Bob Nicholson
123	Bob Sweeney
144	John Meulenbroeks
165	Tony Fiore
186	Doug Kostynski
207	Tony Gilliard
228	Tommy Lehman
249	Bruno Campese

1983

21	Nevin Markwart
42	Greg Johnston
62	Greg Puhalski
82	Allan LaRochelle
102	Allen Pedersen
122	Terry Taillefer
142	Ian Armstrong
162	Francois Olivier
182	Harri Laurila
202	Paul Fitzsimmons
222	Norm Foster
242	Greg Murphy

1984

19	Dave Pasin
40	Ray Podloski
61	Jeff Cornelius
82	Bob Joyce
103	Mike Bishop
124	Randy Oswald
145	Mark Thietke
166	Don Sweeney
186	Kevin Heffernan
207	John Urbanic
227	Bill Kopecky
248	Jim Newhouse

1985

31	Alain Cote
52	Bill Ranford
73	Jamie Kelly
94	Steve Moore
115	Gord Hynes
136	Per Martinelle
157	Randy Burridge
178	Gord Cruickshank
199	Dave Buda
210	Bob Beers
220	John Byce
241	Marc West

1986

13	Craig Janney
34	Pekka Tirkkonen
76	Dean Hall
97	Matt Pesklewis
118	Garth Premak
139	Paul Beraldo
160	Brian Ferreira
181	Jeff Flaherty
202	Greg Hawgood
223	Steffan Malmqvist
244	Joel Gardner

1987

3	Glen Wesley
14	Stephane Quintal
56	Todd Lalonde
67	Darwin McPherson
77	Matt Del Guidice
98	Ted Donato
119	Matt Glennon
140	Rob Cheevers
161	Chris Winnes
182	Paul Ohman
203	Casey Jones
224	Eric LeMarque
245	Sean Gorman

1988

18	Rob Cimetta
60	Steve Heinze
81	Joe Juneau
102	Daniel Murphy
123	Derek Geary
165	Mark Krys
186	Jon Rohloff
228	Eric Reisman
249	Doug Jones

1989

17	Shayne Stevenson
38	Mike Parson
57	Wes Walz
80	Jackson Penney
101	Mark Montanari
122	Stephen Foster
143	Otto Hascak
164	Rick Allain
185	James Lavish
206	Geoff Simpson
227	David Franzosa

1990

21	Bryan Smolinski
63	Cam Stewart
84	Jerome Buckley
105	Mike Bales
126	Mark Woolf
147	Jim Mackey
168	John Gruden
189	Darren Wetherill
210	Dean Capuano
231	Andy Bezeau
252	Ted Miskolczi

1991

18	Glen Murray
40	Jozef Stumpel
62	Marcel Cousineau
84	Brad Tiley
106	Mariusz Czerkawski
150	Gary Golczewski
172	Jay Moser
194	Daniel Hodge
216	Steve Norton
238	Stephen Lombardi
260	Torsten Kienass

1992

16	Dmitri Kvartalnov
55	Sergei Zholtok
112	Scott Bailey
133	Jiri Dopita
136	Grigori Panteleev
184	Kurt Seher
208	Mattias Timander
232	Chris Crombie
256	Denis Chervyakov
257	Evgeny Pavlov

1993

25	Kevyn Adams
51	Matt Alvey
88	Charles Paquette
103	Shawn Bates
129	Andrei Sapozhnikov
155	Milt Mastad
181	Ryan Golden
207	Hal Gill
233	Joel Prpic

1994

21	Evgeni Ryabchikov
47	Daniel Goneau
99	Eric Nickulas
125	Darren Wright
151	Andre Roy
177	Jeremy Schaefer
229	John Grahame
255	Neil Savary
281	Andrei Yakhanov

1995

9	Kyle McLaren
21	Sean Brown
47	Paxton Schafer
73	Bill McCauley
99	Cameron Mann
151	Yevgeny Shaldybin
177	P.J. Axelsson
203	Sergei Zhukov
229	Jonathon Murphy

1996

8	Johnathan Aitken
45	Henry Kuster
53	Eric Naud
80	Jason Doyle
100	Trent Whitfield
132	Elias Abrahamsson
155	Chris Lane
182	Thomas Brown
208	Bob Prier
234	Anders Soderberg

1997

1	Joe Thornton
8	Sergei Samsonov
27	Ben Clymer
54	Mattias Karlin
63	Lee Goren
81	Karol Bartanus
135	Denis Timofeev
162	Joel Trottier
180	Jim Baxter
191	Antti Laaksonen
218	Eric Van Acker
246	Jay Henderson

1998

48	Jonathan Girard
52	Bobby Allen
78	Peter Nordstrom
135	Andrew Raycroft
165	Ryan Milanovic

1999

21	Nick Boynton
56	Matt Zultek
89	Kyle Wanvig
118	Jaakko Harikkala
147	Seamus Kotyk
179	Donald Choukalos
207	Greg Barber
236	John Cronin
247	Mikko Eloranta
264	Georgy Pujacs

2000

7	Lars Jonsson
27	Martin Samuelsson
37	Andy Hilbert
59	Ivan Huml
66	Tuukka Makela
73	Sergei Zinovjev
103	Brett Nowak
174	Jarno Kultanen
204	Chris Berti
237	Zdenek Kutlak
268	Pavel Kolarik
279	Andreas Lindstrom

2001

19	Shaone Morrisonn
77	Darren McLachlan
111	Matti Kaltiainen
147	Jiri Jakes
179	Andrew Alberts
209	Jordan Sigalet
241	Milan Jurcina
282	Marcel Rodman

2002

29	Hannu Toivonen
56	Vladislav Evseev
130	Jan Kubista
153	Peter Hamerlik
228	Dmitri Utkin
259	Yan Stastny
290	Pavel Frolov

2003

21	Mark Stuart
45	Patrice Bergeron
66	Masi Marjamaki
107	Byron Bitz
118	Frank Rediker
129	Patrik Valcak
153	Mike Brown
183	Nate Thompson
247	Benoit Mondou
277	Kevin Regan

2004

63	David Krejci
64	Martins Karsums
108	Ashton Rome
134	Kris Versteeg
160	Ben Walter
224	Matt Hunwick
255	Anton Hedman

2005

22	Matt Lashoff
39	Petr Kalus
83	Mikko Lehtonen
100	Jonathan Sigalet
106	Vladimir Sobotka
154	Wacey Rabbit
172	Lukas Vantuch
217	Brock Bradford

2006

5	Phil Kessel
37	Yury Alexandrov
50	Milan Lucic
71	Brad Marchand
128	Andrew Bodnarchuk
158	Levi Nelson

2007

8	Zach Hamill
35	Tommy Cross
130	Denis Reul
159	Alain Goulet
169	Radim Ostrcil
189	Jordan Knackstedt

2008

16	Joe Colborne
47	Max Sauve
77	Michael Hutchinson
97	Jamie Arniel
173	Nick Tremblay
197	Mark Goggin

2009

25	Jordan Caron
86	Ryan Button
112	Lane MacDermid
176	Tyler Randell
206	Ben Sexton

2010

2	Tyler Seguin
32	Jared Knight
45	Ryan Spooner
97	Craig Cunningham
135	Justin Florek
165	Zane Gothberg
195	Maxim Chudinov
210	Zach Trotman

Bergeron, Patrice

b. L'Ancienne-Lorette, Quebec, July 24, 1985

Centre—shoots right

6'2"—194 lbs.

Drafted 45th overall by Boston in 2003

By virtue of this Stanley Cup win, Bergeron becomes only the twenty-fifth player to join the Triple Gold Club. He won Olympic gold with Canada in 2010 and World Championship gold in 2004, and now he completes TGC qualification with this Stanley Cup.

Indeed, the twenty-five-year-old is one of the youngest players to accomplish this rare feat, but his rise and success are not surprising, at least not after his rookie season. Bergeron went to Boston's training camp in 2003, at age eighteen, looking only for experience, but he performed so well the coaching staff had no choice but to add him to their NHL roster. He had sixteen goals and thirty-nine points as a rookie, and at season's end he was invited to play for Team Canada at the World Championship. Canada won gold, and he had his first international medal.

The next season was lost to the lockout, so Bergeron played in Providence with the Bruins' AHL affiliate. After Christmas he played for Canada at the U20 tournament, skating on a line with seventeen-year-old Sidney Crosby. The two were sensational together, leading Canada to gold over Alexander Ovechkin and Russia. Bergeron became the first player ever to win a World Championship gold before a U20 gold.

In 2005–06, back in the NHL, he had thirty-one goals and asserted himself as one of the game's great young stars. His career was altered, though, on October 27, 2007, when Randy Jones of Philadelphia hit him from behind into the end boards. Bergeron missed the rest of the season suffering post-concussion syndrome, and when he returned he was a different player. Although he hasn't reached the scoring levels of his sophomore season, he remains a top offensive player for the Bruins with, hopefully, many years of high-quality hockey left in his skates.

Career Statistics	Regular Season					Playoffs				
	GP	G	A	P	Pim	GP	G	A	P	Pim
2003-04 BOS	71	16	23	39	22	7	1	3	4	0
2005-06 BOS	81	31	42	73	22	DNQ				
2006-07 BOS	77	22	48	70	26	DNQ				
2007-08 BOS	10	3	4	7	2	DNP				
2008-09 BOS	64	8	31	39	16	11	0	5	5	11
2009-10 BOS	73	19	33	52	28	13	4	7	11	2
2010-11 BOS	80	22	35	57	26	for 2011 playoff stats see p. 18				
NHL Totals	456	121	216	337	142					

for 2011 playoff stats see p. 18

Boychuk, Johnny

b. Edmonton, Alberta, January 19, 1984

Defence—shoots right

6'2"—225 lbs.

Drafted 61st overall by Colorado in 2002

A big and strong defenceman, Boychuk played four years in the WHL (2000–04), primarily with the Calgary Himtmen, before turning pro. His ascent to the NHL has been very slow and has required patience and fierce determination. He played three years in the minors without getting a hint of NHL action, but in 2007–08 he made his first four appearances in a season otherwise spent in the minors.

In fact, Boychuk played four straight years in the AHL, all with different teams—Hershey, Lowell, Albany, and Lake Erie. He played in his first NHL game for the Avalanche on January 5, 2008, against the New York Islanders, and that summer the Avs traded him to Boston in a roster move that seemed to be of little consequence.

But Boychuk continued to dream the dream. The Bruins used him for only one game in 2008–09, but in the summer of 2009 he signed a one-year contract with the team that was also, more importantly, a one-way deal (meaning he couldn't be demoted to the minors unless he were paid an NHL salary).

Boychuk made the most of his chance and had an even stronger season in 2010–11, becoming an important depth player in the Bruins' lineup. Big and tough, he's not a star cut from Bobby Orr cloth, but the defenceman is effective and solid in his own end, and that, very often, is all a coach can ask for.

Career Statistics	Regular Season					Playoffs				
	GP	G	A	P	Pim	GP	G	A	P	Pim
2007-08 COL	4	0	0	0	0	DNP				
2008-09 BOS	1	0	0	0	0	DNP				
2009-10 BOS	51	5	10	15	43	13	2	4	6	6
2010-11 BOS	69	3	13	16	45	for 2011 playoff stats see p. 18				
NHL Totals	125	8	23	31	88					

Campbell, Gregory

b. London, Ontario, December 17, 1983

Defence—shoots left

6'—190 lbs.

Drafted 67th overall by Florida in 2002

The son of a former hockey player, Gregory learned from an early age what it took to make the NHL. He played junior hockey with the Plymouth Whalers starting in 2000, but before his third year he was traded to the Kitchener Rangers. Campbell thrived with the Rangers, having an excellent regular season, and then leading the team to the Memorial Cup finals where he was the leading scorer. He had been drafted by Florida the previous summer, and after this fine season decided to turn pro.

Campbell played most of the next two seasons in the minors, with San Antonio of the AHL, but he did get into two games with the Panthers to get a taste of NHL hockey. In 2005, he made the team out of training camp, playing sixty-four games in all.

The Panthers considered him a useful player, a third-liner who could hit and fight when need be and chip in with a timely goal, kill penalties, and check. But in the summer of 2010, the team wanted to acquire Boston's first-round draft choice in 2010, and traded Nathan Horton and Campbell for that choice, a third-round selection, as well as Dennis Wideman from the Bruins.

Warming up to a new environment, Campbell had a solid year with the Bruins and took on extra responsibility in the post-season, when his play with the puck became as important as his contributions without.

Career Statistics	Regular Season					Playoffs				
	GP	G	A	P	Pim	GP	G	A	P	Pim
2003-04 FLA	2	0	0	0	5	DNQ				
2005-06 FLA	64	3	6	9	40	DNQ				
2006-07 FLA	79	6	3	9	66	DNQ				
2007-08 FLA	81	5	13	18	72	DNQ				
2008-09 FLA	77	13	19	32	76	DNQ				
2009-10 FLA	60	2	15	17	53	DNQ				
2010-11 BOS	80	13	16	29	93	for 2011 playoff stats see p. 18				
NHL Totals	443	42	72	114	405					

for 2011 playoff stats see p. 18

Chara, Zdeno

b. Trencin, Czechoslovakia (Slovakia), March 18, 1977

Defence—shoots left

6'9"—255 lbs.

Drafted 56th overall by NY Islanders in 1996

The tallest player ever to play in the NHL, Chara is incredibly strong and agile for a defenceman of his size. He played the first four years of his career with the New York Islanders, but big men always take longer to develop and that was especially the case for him. The Islanders weren't a particularly good team, which was good for him because he could learn and grow and make mistakes along the way without damaging his psyche.

Chara's first break came in the summer of 2001, when he was traded to Ottawa. The Senators needed a stud on the blue-line at a time when it was developing into a Stanley Cup contender, and he responded by becoming just that stud. He became an offensive force with a cannon-like shot from the point on the power play. He was a force inside his own blue-line because of his size and strength. And, he moved the puck fearlessly out of his own zone, two or three powerful strides were enough to get the job done most times. He also played nearly half a game night after night.

At the end of his second full season, the Senators went to the Conference Final, but that's as far as they got with him. Chara became an unrestricted free agent in the summer of 2006 and decided not to re-sign with the Senators, who had not traded him at the deadline in the hopes of getting him to stay. Chara opted to go to Boston where he signed a five-year, 37.5 million dollar contract, and he was named the team's captain as well.

If Ottawa represented his maturation into a star player, then Boston represents his mature years at the height of his powers. All aspects of his game which had been honed in Ottawa were now put to good use with the Bruins, and Chara became a dominant player. He won the Norris Trophy in 2008–09, and he has won the hardest shot contest at the All-Star Game festivities for several years running, his windup and blasts frightening defencemen eighty-two games a season.

Despite his size, Chara is a player who tries to avoid being overly aggressive because he knows his strength can hurt others. In the summers he goes home to Slovakia and wrestles with his father to stay in shape, and he also climbed Mount Kilimanjaro in 2008. In 2010, he signed a seven-year contract extension which should take him through the rest of his career and allow him to retire a Bruin.

Career Statistics	Regular Season					Playoffs				
	GP	G	A	P	Pim	GP	G	A	P	Pim
1997-98 NYI	25	0	1	1	50			DNQ		
1998-99 NYI	59	2	6	8	83			DNQ		
1999-00 NYI	65	2	9	11	57			DNQ		
2000-01 NYI	82	2	7	9	157			DNQ		
2001-02 OTT	75	10	13	23	156	10	0	1	1	12
2002-03 OTT	74	9	30	39	116	18	1	6	7	14
2003-04 OTT	79	16	25	41	147	7	1	1	2	8
2005-06 OTT	71	16	27	43	135	10	1	3	4	23
2006-07 BOS	80	11	32	43	100			DNQ		
2007-08 BOS	77	17	34	51	114	7	1	1	2	12
2008-09 BOS	80	19	31	50	95	11	1	3	4	12
2009-10 BOS	80	7	37	44	87	13	2	5	7	29
2010-11 BOS	81	14	30	44	88	for 2011 playoff stats see p. 18				
NHL Totals	928	125	282	407	1,385					

Ference, Andrew

b. Edmonton, Alberta, March 17, 1979

Defence—shoots left

5'11"—189 lbs.

Drafted 208th overall by Pittsburgh in 1997

One of the most outspoken members of the NHL's fraternity, Ference plays with a like honesty on ice as well. He gives 100 per cent and, while not flashy, he gets the job done in his own end as well as any defenceman in the game.

Ference played his entire junior career with Portland in the WHL, but he was by no means a stud on the blue-line. He never played for Canada at U18 or U20 tournaments, and he was a low draft choice in 1997, suggesting a long NHL career was not in the cards. But Ference persevered, and the Pittsburgh Penguins gave him his first chance to play in the big league.

Between 1999 and 2003, Ference split most of his time

between the Penguins and their farm team in Wilkes-Barre, and in the 2001 playoffs he was impressive as the team went to the Conference Final. But the Pens gave up on him in early 2003, sending him to Calgary for nothing more than a third-round draft choice.

In his first full season with the Flames, the team went to the Stanley Cup Final before losing to Tampa Bay in game seven. But during his four years with the Flames, the team went from nearly winning it all to not even qualifying for the playoffs, and in February 2007 he was traded to the Bruins with Chuck Kobasew for Wayne Primeau, Brad Stuart, and a draft choice.

The Bruins got just what they wanted, a physical, reliable, stay-at-home defenceman who could chew up ice time without being a liability. He continues to stir the pot off ice sometimes, with his views on the game and social issues, such as the environment, but his colour away from the rink is as refreshing as his play on it is reliable and effective.

Career Statistics	Regular Season					Playoffs				
	GP	G	A	P	Pim	GP	G	A	P	Pim
1999-00 PIT	30	2	4	6	20	DNP				
2000-01 PIT	36	4	11	15	28	18	3	7	10	16
2001-02 PIT	75	4	7	11	73	DNQ				
2002-03 PIT	22	1	3	4	36	--	--	--	--	--
2002-03 CAL	16	0	4	4	6	DNQ				
2003-04 CAL	72	4	12	16	53	26	0	3	3	25
2005-06 CAL	82	4	27	31	85	7	0	4	4	12
2006-07 CAL	54	2	10	12	66	--	--	--	--	--
2006-07 BOS	26	1	2	3	31	DNQ				
2007-08 BOS	59	1	14	15	50	7	0	4	4	6
2008-09 BOS	47	1	15	16	40	3	0	0	0	4
2009-10 BOS	51	0	8	8	16	13	0	1	1	18
2010-11 BOS	70	3	12	15	60	for 2011 playoff stats see p. 18				
NHL Totals	640	27	129	156	564					

for 2011 playoff stats see p. 18

Hnidy, Shane

b. Neepawa, Manitoba, November 8, 1975

Defence—shoots right

6'2"—204 lbs.

Drafted 173rd overall by Buffalo in 1994

What a success story has been the career of Shane Hnidy. Another low draft choice that the Bruins have put to good use during their Stanley Cup run in 2011, he played five years of junior hockey with little promise of an NHL career. Drafted midway through his years in the WHL by Buffalo, he turned pro in 1996 without having signed with the Sabres or anyone else. Instead, he signed a minor-league contract with Baton Rouge of the ECHL and started his climb.

It wasn't until two years later that the Red Wings signed him and assigned him to Adirondack. Another two years later, still with no NHL action, he was traded to his third NHL team, Ottawa. Hnidy made the Senators in 2000–01 and played fifty-two games, looking to be a big and solid body on the blue-line who could play a physical game.

His career derailed a bit in 2001–02 when an ankle injury forced him out for two-thirds of the season, but he returned as good as ever and stayed with the Sens another year and a half. He was traded to Nashville, though, and that's when his carousel career went into full swing.

Hnidy played for five teams over the course of the next six years, always wanted by some team in need of defensive help, but never being a big part of a team's long-term plans. Still, he was given plenty of ice time wherever he went, from the Predators to Thrashers, and on to the Ducks, Bruins, and Wild. Most of the time his teams didn't make the playoffs or didn't get very far, a cause for change at the best of times.

By the summer of 2010, Hnidy's career seemed over. He was a free agent on July 1, but no one called that day or the next or any other. He continued to train while the season began, but it looked pointless until February 23, 2011, when Bruins GM Peter Chiarelli decided to have another look. After three days of practice, he decided Hnidy could be a valuable asset down the stretch and in the long playoff drive, and Hnidy went from unwanted to Stanley Cup champion in a matter of months.

Career Statistics	Regular Season					Playoffs				
	GP	G	A	P	Pim	GP	G	A	P	Pim
2000-01 OTT	52	3	2	5	84	1	0	0	0	0
2001-02 OTT	33	1	1	2	57	12	1	1	2	12
2002-03 OTT	67	0	8	8	130	1	0	0	0	0
2003-04 OTT	37	0	5	5	72	--	--	--	--	--
2003-04 NAS	9	0	2	2	10	5	0	0	0	6
2005-06 ATL	66	0	3	3	33	DNQ				
2006-07 ATL	72	5	7	12	63	4	1	0	1	0
2007-08 ANA	33	1	2	3	30	--	--	--	--	--
2007-08 BOS	43	1	4	5	41	7	1	1	2	9
2008-09 BOS	65	3	9	12	45	7	1	0	1	0
2009-10 MIN	70	2	12	14	66	DNQ				
2010-11 BOS	3	0	0	0	2	for 2011 playoff stats see p. 18				
NHL Totals	550	16	55	71	633					

Horton, Nathan

b. Welland, Ontario, May 29, 1985

Centre—shoots right

6'2"—229 lbs.

Drafted 3rd overall by Florida in 2003

One of the most skilled players in the NHL, Horton played the first six years of his career in Florida, out of the media limelight and under-appreciated by most hockey fans. But he was drafted third overall for a reason. Only Marc-Andre Fleury (first, Pittsburgh) and Eric Staal (second, Carolina) were chosen ahead of him.

For starters, Horton had an outstanding junior career with Oshawa, starting as a sixteen-year-old and becoming one of the top scorers and playmakers in the OHL. The Panthers were quick to realize his talents and had him on the team only weeks after drafting him.

Horton had fourteen goals in fifty-five games as a rookie, a deceiving total because early in the season he suffered a shoulder injury that doctors said could heal on its own. It didn't, and surgery was later required, so Horton ended up playing much of that year well below his physical best. The pattern occurred the next year as well, during the lockout, when he was playing for San Antonio in the AHL. He suffered another shoulder injury and was again shelved after surgery.

By 2005, though, everything had worked itself out. The lockout was over, Horton was healthy and twenty years old and ready to play some NHL hockey. He responded with a twenty-eight-goal season, and the year after he had thirty-one. Horton then signed a six-year deal with Florida worth twenty-four million dollars, and it seemed his long-term future was with the Panthers.

However, Horton was always rumoured to have been unhappy in Florida, and the Panthers were worried that he was injury prone. In addition to his shoulder, he hurt his knee, finger, and suffered a plethora of other, smaller wounds that saw him miss fifteen and seventeen games in 2008–09 and the following year. And, in all the time he was with the team, the Panthers never made the playoffs.

Both sides seemed happy when Horton was traded to the Bruins in the summer of 2010. Horton responded with a strong and healthy season, and in the playoffs he was sensational. In the opening round against Montreal, he scored in overtime of games five and seven to give the Bruins the series win. In the Conference Final, his late goal was the only one of game seven, advancing the team to the Stanley Cup Final and eliminating Tampa Bay. His playoffs came to a crashing end when he was hit in the head by Aaron Rome early in game three of the Stanley Cup Final against Vancouver.

Career Statistics	Regular Season					Playoffs				
	GP	G	A	P	Pim	GP	G	A	P	Pim
2003-04 FLA	55	14	8	22	57	DNQ				
2005-06 FLA	71	28	19	47	89	DNQ				
2006-07 FLA	82	31	31	62	61	DNQ				
2007-08 FLA	82	27	35	62	85	DNQ				
2008-09 FLA	67	22	23	45	48	DNQ				
2009-10 FLA	65	20	37	57	42	DNQ				
2010-11 BOS	80	26	27	53	85	for 2011 playoff stats see p. 18				
NHL Totals	502	168	180	348	467					

Kaberle, Tomas

b. Rakovnik, Czechoslovakia
(Czech Republic), March 2, 1978

Defence—shoots left

6'1"—214 lbs.

Drafted 204th overall by Toronto in 1996

After eleven and a half seasons and almost 900 games with the Toronto Maple Leafs, it seemed Tomas Kaberle would play his career with the Blue & White. But on February 18, 2011, Bruins general manager Peter Chiarelli acquired Kaberle from the Leafs for top prospect Joe Colborne, a first-round draft choice in 2011, and a conditional second-round draft choice. It was a savvy acquisition given that Kaberle had long been considered one of the best puck-moving defencemen in the league.

Kaberle was one of Toronto's best draft stories, a very late-round selection who proved, even at age twenty,

that he could play in the NHL. He joined a Toronto team that was just developing into a possible Stanley Cup contender, and he logged well over a third of a game's worth of ice time every night. Kaberle also anchored the power play, killed penalties, and proved an excellent passer as well.

But after six successful seasons in the playoffs, the Leafs faltered and missed the playoffs every year from 2006 to the present. Changes had to be made, and GM Brian Burke saw the need for a young prospect and a draft choice, so he made the trade with Boston.

Kaberle fit right in, and although he had some rough patches with the power play, he continued to be impressive in his own end.

In addition to his long NHL career, he has had a distinguished career internationally. He won a gold and silver medal in consecutive World Championships with the Czech Republic, in 2005 and 2006, and also helped his country win bronze at the 2006 Olympics. That was one of three Olympics he has played in (along with 2002 and 2010) which, along with the four World Championships and the 2004 World Cup, highlight his resume.

Career Statistics	Regular Season					Playoffs				
	GP	G	A	P	Pim	GP	G	A	P	Pim
1998-99 TOR	57	4	18	22	12	14	0	3	3	2
1999-00 TOR	82	7	33	40	24	12	1	4	5	0
2000-01 TOR	82	6	39	45	24	11	1	3	4	0
2001-02 TOR	69	10	29	39	2	20	2	8	10	16
2002-03 TOR	82	11	36	47	30	13	0	3	3	6
2003-04 TOR	71	3	28	31	18	DNP				
2005-06 TOR	82	9	58	67	46	DNQ				
2006-07 TOR	74	11	47	58	20	DNQ				
2007-08 TOR	82	8	45	53	22	DNQ				
2008-09 TOR	57	4	27	31	8	DNQ				
2009-10 TOR	82	7	42	49	24	DNQ				
2010-11 TOR	58	3	35	38	16	--	--	--	--	--
2010-11 BOS	24	1	8	9	2	for 2011 playoff stats see p.18				
NHL Totals	902	84	445	529	248					

Kampfer, Steve

b. Ann Arbor, Michigan, September 24, 1988

Defence—shoots right

5'11"—197 lbs.

Drafted 93rd overall by Anaheim in 2007

One of the Bruins' young players who made the transition from college, to the AHL, and then to the NHL, with surprising swiftness, Steve Kampfer has arrived in the right place at the right time.

He was a top prospect as an early teen and opted to play college hockey in the U.S. rather than junior hockey in Canada. As a result, he played two years in the USHL waiting to become NCAA eligible, which happened in 2006. Kampfer played at the University of Michigan under legendary coach Red Berenson, and he was a mid-range draft choice of Anaheim at the end of his second year with the Wolverines.

Kampfer played all four years at U of M and made his pro debut at the end of the season with Providence, Boston's AHL affiliate. He had been traded to Boston by Anaheim on March 2, 2010. Anaheim received only a fourth-round draft choice in return, but Kampfer has proved far more valuable than that.

He started the 2010–11 season in the AHL again, but when Mark Stuart suffered an injury Kampfer was called up as his emergency replacement in early December. Kampfer was, if not a revelation, certainly a player of much greater ability than the Bruins might have at first suspected, and he remained in the lineup the rest of the year. Indeed, the Bruins later traded Stuart to Atlanta, knowing Kampfer was a capable substitute.

Not big, Kampfer relies on steady and reliable play to make his reputation. He won't overpower opponents, but he can outsmart them and he moves the puck especially well. Only twenty-two, the future is bright for the young star who is still learning as he goes.

Career Statistics	Regular Season					Playoffs				
	GP	G	A	P	Pim	GP	G	A	P	Pim
2010-11 BOS	38	5	5	10	12	for 2011 playoff stats see p. 18				

Kelly, Chris

b. Toronto, Ontario, November 11, 1980

Centre—shoots left

6'—198 lbs.

Drafted 94th overall by Ottawa in 1999

A prototypical utility player, no team can win the Stanley Cup without a Chris Kelly in the lineup. He can check, kill penalties, skate hard, block shots, and play the team's system, all elements of winning hockey.

Kelly played fully four seasons in the OHL, mostly with the dominant London Knights, from 1997 to 2001. Midway through his junior career he was drafted by the Ottawa Senators, and it was with that team he started his NHL career in 2001, playing for the team's AHL affiliate in Grand Rapids.

His was not a meteoric rise, though. Kelly spent most of the next four years in the minors, working on his game and waiting patiently for the chance to be called up. He played four games for the Sens in 2003–04, but the next year was lost to the lockout and he was back in the minors. It wasn't until training camp in 2005, fully six years after his name was called at the draft, that Kelly became a bona fide NHLer. He immediately fit in with the team, though, and was part of the run to the Stanley Cup Final in 2007 when the Sens lost in five games to Anaheim.

The Senators and Bruins were moving in opposite directions in 2010–11, and it's for those reasons he switched teams. The Sens were clearly not going to make the playoffs while the Bruins were preparing for a long run, so they acquired Kelly near the deadline for a second-round draft choice in 2011.

Indeed, it was a brilliant acquisition. Kelly was outstanding in the post-season, doing nothing flashy but doing everything needed to get the team the Stanley Cup. His best moment came in game four of the first round when he had a goal and two assists in helping defeat the Canadiens 5–4 and even that series, which was eventually won by the Bruins in seven games.

Career Statistics	Regular Season					Playoffs				
	GP	G	A	P	Pim	GP	G	A	P	Pim
2003-04 OTT	4	0	0	0	0	DNP				
2005-06 OTT	82	10	20	30	76	10	0	0	0	2
2006-07 OTT	82	15	23	38	40	20	3	4	7	4
2007-08 OTT	75	11	19	30	30	DNP				
2008-09 OTT	82	12	11	23	38	DNQ				
2009-10 OTT	81	15	17	32	38	6	1	5	6	2
2010-11 OTT	57	12	11	23	27	--	--	--	--	--
2010-11 BOS	24	2	3	5	6	for 2011 playoff stats see p. 18				
NHL Totals	487	77	104	181	255					

for 2011 playoff stats see p. 18

Krejci, David

b. Sternberk, Czechoslovakia
(Czech Republic), April 28, 1986

Centre—shoots right

6'—177 lbs.

Drafted 63rd overall by Boston in 2004

One of the best of a new crop of Czech players to make it to the NHL, Krejci has quickly made his mark on this Boston Bruins team. His skill around the enemy net is undeniable, and his timely scoring and ability to come up big are also an important part of the Bruins' success this year.

It was while he was still playing in the Czech Republic that Bruins' scouts felt an admiration for Krejci. After drafting him in 2004, they convinced him to play junior hockey to allow him to adapt to the North American game, and he started a two-year career with Gatineau in the QMJHL. He had two solid years and then advanced to the next level, playing for Providence of the AHL.

It was during this time that he got into his first NHL games. The first came on January 30, 2007, against Buffalo, but after six games he was back in the minors for the rest of the year. Not so in 2007–08. Although he started again in Providence, he was recalled by the Bruins and never left.

The next year, his first full season, he had twenty-two goals, and although he hasn't yet reached that number again, he has proved a capable NHLer. In the 2011 playoffs, he was the dominant player in game six of the Conference Final against Tampa Bay, scoring three times in a 5–4 overtime loss. In the critical games three and four of the Final, the Bruins trailing and needing to win both games, he had two points in both games, 8–1 and 4–0 victories. Krejci is skilled with the puck and was among the ice-time leaders in the 2011 playoffs, a vital part of his team's Stanley Cup success.

Career Statistics	Regular Season					Playoffs				
	GP	G	A	P	Pim	GP	G	A	P	Pim
2006-07 BOS	6	0	0	0	2	DNQ				
2007-08 BOS	56	6	21	27	20	7	1	4	5	2
2008-09 BOS	82	22	51	73	26	11	2	6	8	2
2009-10 BOS	79	17	35	52	26	9	4	4	8	2
2010-11 BOS	75	13	49	62	28	for 2011 playoff stats see p. 18				
NHL Totals	298	58	156	214	102					

Lucic, Milan

b. Vancouver, British Columbia, June 7, 1988

Left wing—shoots left

6'4"—220 lbs.

Drafted 50th overall by Boston in 2006

Was there any player in a more difficult position than Milan Lucic throughout the Stanley Cup Final? He was, after all, a Vancouver native and was a hero in the city for his junior career. But there he was, with the Bruins, taking the Cup from his hometown and winning it for another city.

Lucic played his junior hockey with the Vancouver Giants, and his two years with the team culminated in the spring of 2007 when he led the team to an incredible victory in the Memorial Cup, beating Medicine Hat, 3–1, in the championship game. Lucic was named tournament MVP and was a hero, the local boy of immigrant parents leading his team to a stunning junior title.

As a result of his play and leadership, Lucic was named captain for Canada's eight-game Super Series meeting at the U20 level with the Russians that fall, a dominating win by Canada (seven victories, one tie).

Lucic had been drafted by Boston the previous year, but fans had no idea how fortuitous that would be just a few years later. Lucic made the Bruins in the fall of 2007 at age nineteen, and was an instant success for his skating, hitting, intensity, and enthusiasm. The Bruins decided to keep him for the season rather than return him to junior, and he hasn't looked back. Like a larger Wendel Clark, he established himself first with his fists, and then with his scoring, the former giving him more room to perform the latter. His eight goals as a rookie turned into seventeen a year later, and his energy on ice and in the dressing room were infectious.

Lucic missed more than a quarter of the 2009–10 season with injury and the season ended in shocking disappointment for the team. Ahead 3–0 in games against Philadelphia in the Conference Semi-Final, the Flyers rallied and eliminated the Bruins in seven games. The loss, while devastating, helped the Bruins defeat that same team during their Stanley Cup run in 2011. In the team's 5–1 win over Philadelphia to eliminate the Flyers in 2011, Lucic scored two goals and was a key player throughout the playoffs for using his size and strength without taking bad penalties or putting his team short-handed.

If the Bruins are going to continue their winning ways for years ahead, it will do so with Lucic in the lineup. A hero from Vancouver, he spoiled the Canucks party but still made the people of British Columbia proud of him.

Career Statistics	Regular Season						Playoffs				
	GP	G	A	P	Pim		GP	G	A	P	Pim
2007-08 BOS	77	8	19	27	89		7	2	0	2	4
2008-09 BOS	72	17	25	42	136		10	3	6	9	43
2009-10 BOS	50	9	11	20	44		13	5	4	9	19
2010-11 BOS	79	30	32	62	121		for 2011 playoff stats see p. 18				
NHL Totals	278	64	87	151	390						

for 2011 playoff stats see p. 18

Marchand, Brad

b. Halifax, Nova Scotia, May 11, 1988

Centre—shoots left

5'9"—183 lbs.

Drafted 71st overall by Boston in 2006

A young player who is just getting better and better, Brad Marchand is the foundation upon which the Bruins can build a future. He had four excellent seasons in junior with the QMJHL, developing into a better player than his seventy-first overall draft selection halfway through his junior career indicated.

At the same time he was playing with Moncton and Val d'Or, Marchand also played for Canada at the U20 championship, in both 2007 and 2008, helping the team win gold both times. He then went to Providence for the entire 2008–09 season and learned the pro game. The following year he split between the Bruins (20 games) and Providence (34).

Marchand made the NHL in 2010 at training camp and became a sensational player, one of the most talked-about rookies. Among his twenty-one goals, five were short-handed, and both numbers placed him among the best of the first-year players. In the 2011 playoffs, he continued to score timely and important goals.

He opened the scoring in game five against Montreal in the first round. He had two goals and an assist in the opener against Philadelphia to get the team off on the right note. And, he got the game winner in game five against Tampa Bay. He also scored goals in games three and four of the Final against Vancouver. Every round he did something important for the team.

Career Statistics	Regular Season					Playoffs				
	GP	G	A	P	Pim	GP	G	A	P	Pim
2009-10 BOS	20	0	1	1	20	DNP				
2010-11 BOS	77	21	20	41	51	for 2011 playoff stats see p. 18				
NHL Totals	97	21	21	42	71					

McQuaid, Adam

b. Charlottetown, Prince Edward Island, October 12, 1986

Defence—shoots right

6'5"—209 lbs.

Drafted 55th overall by Columbus in 2005

A towering defenceman with loads of potential, Adam McQuaid might well have been a steal of a deal for the Bruins. He was drafted by Columbus after his second year with the Sudbury Wolves in the OHL. After two more years there, the Blue Jackets decided he wasn't going to be a part of their future. They traded him to Boston for no more than a fifth-round draft choice in 2007.

McQuaid was immediately assigned to the Bruins farm team in Providence and told to work on improving every aspect of his game, and not to think about the NHL for the near future. The taller they are, the slower they develop, is a tried and true motto, and it served McQuaid well. For two full seasons he had nothing to do with the Bruins, but in 2009–10, his progress impressive, the Bruins called him up and he ended up splitting his season between the NHL and AHL.

In 2010–11 he played exclusively for the Bruins and developed into a Zdeno Chara type defenceman. Big and strong, he used his size for all it was worth, but he also stayed out of the penalty box when it mattered the most, namely the 2011 playoffs. McQuaid averaged about 12–14 minutes of ice time a game, but he was only a minus player once all post-season, and was an important presence when the Final series against the Canucks got rough.

Still only twenty-four and a little raw around the edges, McQuaid shows the potential to keep getting better—and bigger and stronger—not something opposing forwards want to hear.

Career Statistics	Regular Season					Playoffs				
	GP	G	A	P	Pim	GP	G	A	P	Pim
2009-10 BOS	19	1	0	1	21	9	0	0	0	6
2010-11 BOS	67	3	12	15	96	for 2011 playoff stats see p. 18				
NHL Totals	86	4	12	16	117					

for 2011 playoff stats see p. 18

Paille, Daniel

b. Welland, Ontario, April 15, 1984

Left wing—shoots left

6'1"—200 lbs.

Drafted 20th overall by Buffalo in 2002

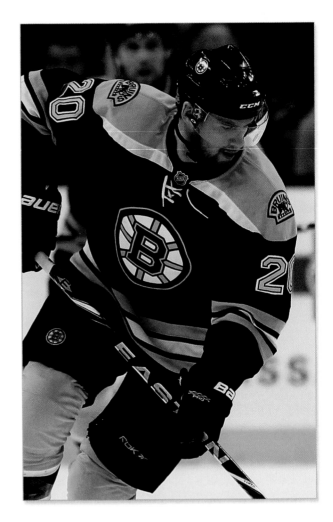

A first-round draft choice by Buffalo, Daniel Paille had excellent credentials coming out of junior hockey. He played four years with the Guelph Storm (2000–04), during which time he also played for Canada twice at the World U20 (Junior) Championship, winning a silver medal both years.

After graduating from the OHL in 2004, Paille went to the Sabres' AHL farm team in Rochester for the better part of two years, but he slowly worked his way into the Sabres' field of vision. In 2005–06, he played his first fourteen NHL games, and the year after he split his time evenly between the Americans and Sabres.

In 2007, Paille made the team and had a fine season, scoring nineteen goals and recording a plus-9 on a team that missed the playoffs. His production dipped the next year, though, and on October 20, 2009, he was traded to the Bruins for a third-round draft choice in 2010. It was the first ever trade between the two teams involving roster players.

Paille has been a versatile, third-line player with the Bruins, very strong defensively while chipping in with the occasional goal or big play in the offensive end.

Career Statistics	Regular Season					Playoffs				
	GP	G	A	P	Pim	GP	G	A	P	Pim
2005-06 BUF	14	1	2	3	2	DNP				
2006-07 BUF	29	3	8	11	18	1	0	0	0	0
2007-08 BUF	77	19	16	35	14	DNQ				
2008-09 BUF	73	12	15	27	20	DNQ				
2009-10 BUF	2	0	1	1	0	--	--	--	--	--
2009-10 BOS	74	10	9	19	12	13	0	2	2	2
2010-11 BOS	43	6	7	13	28	for 2011 playoff stats see p. 18				
NHL Totals	312	51	58	109	94					

for 2011 playoff stats see p. 18

Peverley, Rich

b. Guelph, Ontario, July 8, 1982

Centre—shoots right

6'—195 lbs.

Undrafted

If ever there was a story of determination and will, it is the Rich Peverley story. He was never a top prospect or outstanding teen player, so when he was drafted by Mississauga in the OHL in 1999, he decided to play provincial hockey for a year instead so that he could attend St. Lawrence on an NCAA scholarship.

Peverley had plenty of skill, but there was nothing that stood out to attract agents to him. He was solid, but not really big. A fine skater, he was an impressive offensive player without being flashy. The result was that through his four years with the Skating Saints (the nickname of St. Lawrence), he was never drafted and never even signed as a free agent by any of the thirty NHL teams.

In 2004, with no options other than those of his own choosing, he signed with South Carolina of the ECHL. The year after he had made his way up to the AHL, with Milwaukee, and midway through the 2006–07 he signed a contract with the Nashville Predators. He played thirteen games with the team in what was otherwise an AHL season, and managed only a single assist in that short stint.

Peverley split the next year between the AHL and NHL again, but the year after the Predators put him on waivers. Atlanta claimed him and in thirty-nine games with the Thrashers he had an impressive thirteen goals. In 2009–10, his first bona fide full NHL season, Peverley had twenty-two goals and fifty-five points, pretty near star numbers considering his hockey pedigree to this point.

Then, late in the 2010–11 season, Atlanta traded him and Boris Valabik to Boston for Mark Stuart and Blake Wheeler. The rest, as they say, is history.

Career Statistics	Regular Season					Playoffs				
	GP	G	A	P	Pim	GP	G	A	P	Pim
2006-07 NAS	13	0	1	1	0	DNP				
2007-08 NAS	33	5	5	10	8	6	0	2	2	0
2008-09 NAS	27	2	7	9	15	--	--	--	--	--
2008-09 ATL	39	13	22	35	18	DNQ				
2009-10 ATL	82	22	33	55	36	DNQ				
2010-11 ATL	59	14	20	34	35	--	--	--	--	--
2010-11 BOS	23	4	3	7	2	for 2011 playoff stats see p. 18				
NHL Totals	276	60	91	151	114					

for 2011 playoff stats see p. 18

Rask, Tuukka

b. Savonlinna, Finland, March 10, 1987

Goalie—catches left

6'3"—169 lbs.

Drafted 21st overall by Toronto in 2005

It seems like a long time ago now, but there was a time when the Toronto Maple Leafs had two excellent goalies in their system thanks to their draft—Justin Pogge and Tuukka Rask. The Leafs decided that Pogge was the goalie of their future and traded Rask to Boston on June 24, 2006, for another goalie Andrew Raycroft. Well, the Leafs lost out because Pogge never panned out, and neither did Raycroft. Rask did.

Drafted at eighteen, Rask played two more years in Finland before coming to Boston in the fall of 2007. He was assigned to Providence out of training camp and over the course of the season was called up to play four games. The next year, he played just once for the Bruins, but at camp in 2009, he proved to be the second best goalie after number-one man Tim Thomas.

As it turned out, Thomas struggled a bit that year and Rask filled in more than ably, playing forty-five games and recording a goals-against average of a sensational 1.97. Indeed, he took the starter's role from Thomas for the playoffs, appearing in every minute of every game for the Bruins. The team lost to Philadelphia in seven games in the second round, though, and by training camp 2010 Thomas was back as the number-one goalie.

Nevertheless, Rask has proved an excellent backup, a goalie who doesn't mind playing fewer games than the starter but who is capable of playing well when called upon. He and Thomas form one of the best goalie duos in the game for this very reason, but just as Thomas didn't play in the 2010 playoffs, so, too, didn't Rask play in 2011 because his partner was so dominating.

Career Statistics			Regular Season					Playoffs					
	GP	W-L-O/T	Mins	GA	SO	GAA		GP	W-L	Mins	GA	SO	GAA
2007-08 BOS	4	2-1-1	184	10	0	3.26				DNP			
2008-09 BOS	1	1-0-0	60	0	1	0.00				DNP			
2009-10 BOS	45	22-12-5	2,562	84	5	1.97		13	7-6	829	36	0	.910
2010-11 BOS	29	11-14-2	1,594	71	2	2.67				for 2011 playoff stats see p. 18			
NHL Totals	79	36-27-8	4,401	165	8	2.25							

for 2011 playoff stats see p. 18

Recchi, Mark

b. Kamloops, British Columbia, February 1, 1968

Right wing—shoots left

5'10"—195 lbs.

Drafted 67th overall by Pittsburgh in 1988

The oldest player in the NHL at forty-three and a sure hall of famer three years after he retires, Mark Recchi is the inspiration that gets many of his teammates going. His experience is of such value he's like an extra assistant coach, and his incredible success means that players respect him and listen to his every word.

Incredibly, Recchi played junior between 1984 and 1988, his early career culminating in 1988 when he helped Canada win gold at the U20 championship. He joined Pittsburgh that fall and was with the team for four years, winning his first Stanley Cup in 1991. Midway through the next season he was traded to Philadelphia, and soon he was playing on the famous Legion of Doom line with Eric Lindros and Mikael Renberg. This became the most dominant line in the game, one that defined its era for featuring three power forwards who were incredibly strong on the puck, but who also had goal scorer's hands around the net.

Recchi had long stints with the Flyers twice (1991–95 and 1998–2004), squeezed around five years in Montreal, and three times he had seasons of at least 107 points during the prime of his career. In 1992–93, he also had fifty-three goals, the only time he has reached that plateau in his career.

Since the lockout, though, Recchi has been an itinerant player, playing for five teams and having success wherever he has been. He was a veteran presence with Carolina in 2006 when the Hurricanes won the Stanley Cup, but he has been with the Bruins since being traded by Tampa Bay in March 2009. It seems to have been a perfect match for Recchi.

He still possesses fine hands around the goal, and in the Stanley Cup Final against Vancouver, he became the oldest player ever to score in a Stanley Cup Final game when he scored in game two, a loss. He came right back and scored twice in the team's decisive 8–1 win, and he continued to log fifteen minutes or more of ice time every game. By winning his third career Cup in 2011, he also has the rare distinction of having won those three in different decades.

Career Statistics	Regular Season					Playoffs				
	GP	G	A	P	Pim	GP	G	A	P	Pim
1988-89 PIT	15	1	1	2	0			DNP		
1989-90 PIT	74	30	37	67	44			DNQ		
1990-91 PIT	78	40	73	113	48	24	10	24	34	33
1991-92 PIT	58	33	37	70	78	--	--	--	--	--
1991-92 PHI	22	10	17	27	18			DNQ		
1992-93 PHI	84	53	70	123	95			DNQ		
1993-94 PHI	84	40	67	107	46			DNQ		
1994-95 PHI	10	2	3	5	12	--	--	--	--	--
1994-95 MON	39	14	29	43	16			DNQ		
1995-96 MON	82	28	50	78	69	6	3	3	6	0
1996-97 MON	82	34	46	80	58	5	4	2	6	2
1997-98 MON	82	32	42	74	51	10	4	8	12	6
1998-99 MON	61	12	35	47	28	--	--	--	--	--
1998-99 PHI	10	4	2	6	6	6	0	1	1	2
1999-00 PHI	82	28	63	91	50	18	6	12	18	6
2000-01 PHI	69	27	50	77	33	6	2	2	4	2
2001-02 PHI	80	22	42	64	46	4	0	0	0	2
2002-03 PHI	79	20	32	52	35	13	7	3	10	2
2003-04 PHI	82	26	49	75	47	18	4	2	6	4
2005-06 PIT	63	24	33	57	56	--	--	--	--	--
2005-06 CAR	20	4	3	7	12	25	7	9	16	18
2006-07 PIT	82	24	44	68	62	5	0	4	4	0
2007-08 PIT	19	2	6	8	12	--	--	--	--	--
2007-08 ATL	53	12	28	40	20			DNQ		
2008-09 TB	62	13	32	45	20	--	--	--	--	--
2008-09 BOS	18	10	6	16	2	11	3	3	6	2
2009-10 BOS	81	18	25	43	34	13	6	4	10	6
2010-11 BOS	81	14	34	48	35	for 2011 playoff stats see p. 18				
NHL Totals	1,652	577	956	1,533	1,033					

for 2011 playoff stats see p. 18

Ryder, Michael

b. St. John's, Newfoundland, March 31, 1980

Right wing—shoots right

6'—192 lbs.

Drafted 216th overall by Montreal in 1998

Another in a series of low round draft choices who have ended up playing key roles for the Bruins, Michael Ryder vaulted into the limelight with the Montreal Canadiens in 2003. He had had an excellent junior career with Hull in the QMJHL, but despite taking the Olympiques to the Memorial Cup finals, it was still five years after being drafted that he made his NHL debut. He ended his junior career helping Canada win bronze at the 2000 U20 Championship.

After leaving Hull in 2000, he spent the next three years entirely in the minors, even spending good chunks of time in the ECHL, a league below the AHL and far removed from the glory of the NHL. Ryder had a great year with Hamilton in 2002–03, though, scoring thirty-four goals and helping the team reach the Calder Cup finals. He even scored the overtime winner in the fourth overtime of a game against Houston, the longest game in AHL history.

In his rookie season, Ryder had twenty-five goals and looked to be a scoring sensation in the making. The lockout slowed him down for a season, during which time he played in Sweden, and when the NHL resumed play, Ryder had consecutive thirty-goal seasons. Just when it seemed like his worth was going to go through the ceiling, he followed with a fourteen-goal season and became a free agent. The Habs thought his best days were behind him, and Ryder looked elsewhere, signing with the Bruins for three years. The coach of Boston was now Claude Julien, who had been Ryder's coach in the AHL and with the Canadiens, and he recommended Ryder to the Bruins.

Although he has yet to reach thirty goals again, Ryder has been a valuable and effective player for the Bruins. He scored the overtime winner in game four of the opening round against Montreal, tying the series at a time the Habs could have taken a commanding 3–1 lead. Ryder also scored twice in game two against Tampa Bay, helping the Bruins even that series, which they eventually won in seven games. He also had two key assists in the second period of game three against Vancouver en route to an easy, but vital win in the Final.

Career Statistics	Regular Season					Playoffs				
	GP	G	A	P	Pim	GP	G	A	P	Pim
2003-04 MON	81	25	38	65	26	11	1	2	3	4
2005-06 MON	81	30	25	55	40	6	2	3	5	0
2006-07 MON	82	30	28	58	60	DNQ				
2007-08 MON	70	14	17	31	30	4	0	0	0	2
2008-09 BOS	74	27	26	53	26	11	5	8	13	8
2009-10 BOS	82	18	15	33	35	13	4	1	5	2
2010-11 BOS	79	18	23	41	26	for 2011 playoff stats see p. 18				
NHL Totals	549	162	172	334	243					

Savard, Marc

b. Ottawa, Ontario, July 17, 1977

Centre—shoots left

5'10"—191 lbs.

Drafted 91st overall by NY Rangers in 1995

One of the finest playmakers in the game today, Marc Savard now finds his career in jeopardy after he suffered two serious concussions in less than a year. This, despite his incredible skill, which has allowed him to average nearly a point a game during his thirteen-year career.

Savard had a superb junior career with Oshawa (1993–97), twice leading the OHL in scoring. He was an excellent skater and passer, but his defensive skills were thought to be his nemesis, which is why, despite his tremendous offence, he never played for Canada at the U20 tournament. Still, he made the Rangers in 1997 at age twenty, although he played more in the AHL with Hartford that year than with the Blueshirts.

The year after, he was mostly with the Rangers, but they didn't think he fit into

their system and traded him to Calgary at the Entry Draft in 1999. Savard showed only moderate promise with the Flames, though he did have back-to-back twenty-goal seasons. But every year in the league he had been a minus player in the plus-minus stats, a fact that harmed his reputation, despite his offensive skills.

The Flames traded him to Atlanta on November 15, 2002, for Ruslan Zainullin, and it was with the Thrashers, playing on a line with Ilya Kovalchuk and Dany Heatley, that he developed into a true star. In his only full season he had twenty-eight goals and ninety-seven points, but in the summer of 2006 he became an unrestricted free agent and signed with Boston. The four-year deal worth twenty million dollars was the largest of his career, and he responded with several excellent seasons, averaging better than a point a game.

But on March 7, 2010, Pittsburgh's Matt Cooke hit Savard in the head from the back side and knocked him unconscious. Savard was carried off the ice on a stretcher and missed the rest of the season, and this past year he suffered another concussion after only twenty-five games, which ended his season again.

Career Statistics	Regular Season					Playoffs				
	GP	G	A	P	Pim	GP	G	A	P	Pim
1997-98 NYR	28	1	5	6	4	DNQ				
1998-99 NYR	70	9	36	45	38	DNQ				
1999-00 CAL	78	22	31	53	56	DNQ				
2000-01 CAL	77	23	42	65	46	DNQ				
2001-02 CAL	56	14	19	33	48	DNQ				
2002-03 CAL	10	1	2	3	8	--	--	--	--	--
2002-03 ATL	57	16	31	47	77	DNQ				
2003-04 ATL	45	19	33	52	85	DNQ				
2005-06 ATL	82	28	69	97	100	DNQ				
2006-07 BOS	82	22	74	96	96	DNQ				
2007-08 BOS	74	15	63	78	66	7	1	5	6	6
2008-09 BOS	82	25	63	88	70	11	6	7	13	4
2009-10 BOS	41	10	23	33	14	7	1	2	3	12
2010-11 BOS	25	2	8	10	29	DNP				
NHL Totals	807	207	499	706	737					

Seguin, Tyler

b. Brampton, Ontario, January 31, 1992

Centre—shoots right

6'1"—186 lbs.

Drafted 2nd overall by Boston in 2010

Few players need only two years of major junior hockey before they are ready for the NHL, but Tyler Seguin was one of them. He was a dominating player with the Plymouth Whalers in 2009–10, his second season, leading all scorers in the OHL and being named the league's best player. On draft day, it was a fight between him and Taylor Hall of the Windsor Spitfires. In the end, Edmonton took Hall and the Bruins took Seguin.

Seguin was clearly the real deal. Not the biggest or strongest player, he had great speed and a good shot and proved at his first training camp in 2011 that he could play with the big boys. He scored a goal in his second career game and had eleven on the season, by no means spectacular numbers, but numbers dictated in part by his limited ice time.

Coach Claude Julien made it clear to him that his rookie season was as much about watching and learning as about playing twenty-three minutes a game. Every now and then he showed the team a move or play that indicated his skill set, but he was still young and raw with plenty of time to learn—and he showed a willingness to be patient.

That patience was tested in the 2011 playoffs. Seguin, who had played seventy-four games in the regular season, found himself a healthy scratch for all the games in the first two rounds against Montreal and Philadelphia. But Julien felt the time was right to play him, and Seguin was in the lineup for every game of the Tampa Bay series. In his first playoff game, he had a goal and assist in a 5–2 loss to the Lightning, but in game two he single-handedly carried the team to victory, scoring two goals (one of the highlight-reel variety) and two assists in a decisive 6–5 win.

Everyone used the term "coming-out party" to describe this game, but Seguin wasn't a factor the rest of the series. No matter, he contributed to one huge win, and continued to watch and learn. He'll be a star in the league, of that there can be little doubt, but the Bruins want to make sure he gets there the right way.

Career Statistics	Regular Season					Playoffs				
	GP	G	A	P	Pim	GP	G	A	P	Pim
2010-11 BOS	74	11	11	22	18	for 2011 playoff stats see p. 18				

for 2011 playoff stats see p. 18

Seidenberg, Dennis

b. Schwenningen, West Germany (Germany), July 18, 1981

Defence—shoots left

6'1"—210 lbs.

Drafted 172nd overall by Philadelphia in 2001

One of the studs on the Boston blue-line, Dennis Seidenberg is a dominant defenceman, both for the Bruins and for his country. He has no interest in creating offence and rushing the puck like Bobby Orr, but inside his own blue-line, there are few players of equal value in the league.

Seidenberg played his teen hockey for Adler Mannheim in the DEL (German first division), and just before his twentieth birthday he was drafted by Philadelphia. He stayed one more year in Mannheim and then decided to give pro hockey in North America a go, and for the next three years that meant playing mainly in the minors.

In 2002–03, his rookie season, Seidenberg was mostly an NHLer, but he suffered a leg injury midway through the next season and missed half a year. The lockout forced him to play solely with the Philadelphia Phantoms in the AHL, but it was tremendous learning

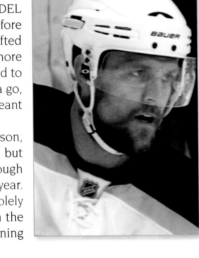

experience for him and he helped the team win the Calder Cup. Ever since then, he has been in the NHL.

No sooner had the lockout ended than the Flyers traded him to Phoenix, and the next year the Coyotes traded him again, shipping him to Carolina. Two and a half seasons later, he found himself an unwanted free agent, and it was Florida that signed him at training camp in 2009 after he appeared as a special invitation.

Again that season he was traded, this time to the Bruins, and he has found a second life in Boston. Under Claude Julien, Seidenberg has logged as much ice time as any player, seeing extra time against the best lines of other teams, killing penalties, blocking shots, and taking care of business in his own end. In the 2011 playoffs, only three times did he fail to log twenty-five minutes of ice time, a compliment from the coaching staff which shows their trust in him.

Also, he has represented Germany at three Olympics and three World Championships, as well as the 2004 World Cup. He is as revered in his native Germany as he is by the Boston fans, who appreciate his professionalism and dedication to the team he plays for, whatever and wherever that may be.

Career Statistics	Regular Season					Playoffs				
	GP	G	A	P	Pim	GP	G	A	P	Pim
2002-03 PHI	58	4	9	13	20	DNP				
2003-04 PHI	5	0	0	0	2	3	0	0	0	0
2005-06 PHI	29	2	5	7	4	DNP				
2005-06 PHO	34	1	10	11	14	DNQ				
2006-07 PHO	32	1	1	2	16	DNQ				
2006-07 CAR	20	1	5	6	2	DNQ				
2007-08 CAR	47	0	15	15	18	DNQ				
2008-09 CAR	70	5	25	30	37	16	1	5	6	16
2009-10 FLA	62	2	21	23	33	--	--	--	--	--
2009-10 BOS	17	2	7	9	6	DNP				
2010-11 BOS	81	7	25	32	41	for 2011 playoff stats see p. 18				
NHL Totals	455	25	123	148	193					

for 2011 playoff stats see p. 18

Thomas, Tim

b. Flint, Michigan, April 15, 1974

Goalie—catches left

5'11"—201 lbs.

Drafted 217th overall by Quebec in 1994

Few goalies in the game's history have taken the path to greatness that Tim Thomas has, and few have peaked at age thirty-seven as he has this 2010–11 season. Incredibly, he was drafted so long ago that it was the Quebec Nordiques that first owned his rights, but they took him so low, 217th overall, no one would have thought Thomas would be anything but a small footnote in that draft, let alone make the annals of NHL history.

Thomas played goal at the University of Vermont for four years (1993–97) where one of his teammates was Martin St. Louis, another late bloomer who was so under-appreciated that he wasn't even drafted. But Thomas was never signed by Quebec and was left to his own devices. He played in the minors a bit and then went to Finland to play with IFK Helsinki where he had a sensational year.

This led to one real offer back home, a contract with Edmonton to play for the farm team in Hamilton. Thomas signed, grew unhappy quickly, and went back to Finland. In all, he played five years in Finland and Sweden and three more years in the AHL before he got anything close to a decent chance to play in the NHL. The Bruins had given him four games in 2002–03, so he signed with them again in 2005 and finally started a career towards the NHL.

In that first season he split his time between the NHL Bruins and Providence, but thereafter he was the starting goalie for Boston most nights. In 2008–09 he won the Vezina Trophy and shared the William Jennings Trophy (with backup Manny Fernandez), but in the 2011 playoffs he started to play at a level he had never achieved before. Confident and cocky, he played outside his crease to cut down angles, and he never allowed those heart-breaking bad goals that can let a team down or allow the opposition the chance to get back into a game.

Thomas is a bona fide American goalie who developed in Finland, matured in his thirties, and might now be the best goalie in the NHL at age thirty-seven.

Career Statistics		Regular Season						Playoffs					
	GP	W-L-O/T	Mins	GA	SO	GAA		GP	W-L	Mins	GA	SO	GAA
2002-03 BOS	4	3-1-0	220	11	0	3.01		DNP					
2005-06 BOS	38	12-13-10	2,1987	101	1	2.77		DNQ					
2006-07 BOS	66	30-29-4	3,619	189	3	3.13		DNQ					
2007-08 BOS	57	28-19-6	3,342	136	3	2.44		7	3-4	430	19	0	2.65
2008-09 BOS	54	36-11-7	3,259	114	5	2.10		11	7-4	680	21	1	1.85
2009-10 BOS	43	17-18-8	2,442	104	5	2.56		DNP					
2010-11 BOS	57	35-11-9	3,364	112	9	2.00		for 2011 playoff stats see p. 18					
NHL Totals	319	161-102-44	18,432	767	26	2.50							

Thornton, Shawn

b. Oshawa, Ontario, July 23, 1977

Right wing—shoots right

6'2"—217 lbs.

Drafted 190th overall by Toronto in 1997

It isn't very often a team's enforcer gets quality ice time in the playoffs, but Shawn Thornton has proved to be much more than just a puncher and policeman for the Boston Bruins. That coach Claude Julien had the confidence to dress him in most of the team's playoff games during their Cup run of 2011 indicates the confidence the coach had in him, but that was not always the case.

Thornton racked up some colossal penalty minutes during his days in junior and the minors. After two years in Peterborough, the Leafs drafted him in 1997 and he immediately turned pro, reporting to Toronto's farm team in St. John's that fall. But in four years in the minors he didn't get a single shift in the NHL, although he averaged some 300 penalty minutes every season.

Toronto traded him to Chicago for Marty Wilford, a minor-league deal that had little consequence to the greater meaning of life. But over the course of the next four years Thornton did manage to play thirty-one games for the Blackhawks, realizing his dream of making it to the NHL. Even better, he signed with Anaheim as a free agent in the summer of 2006, and at the end of the season he found himself on the Stanley Cup–winning team.

He had played forty-eight regular-season games with the team and fifteen more in the playoffs, but the Ducks chose not to re-sign him and the Bruins stepped up. Thornton has been with the B's ever since, and has never played in the minors for the team. As if showing his appreciation, he had a career year in 2010–11 with ten goals and twenty points, but he also knew his job was to protect the players who were paid to put the puck in the net. Thornton has always been the consummate team player, never the most skilled, but never one whom could be criticized for lack of effort.

Career Statistics	Regular Season					Playoffs				
	GP	G	A	P	Pim	GP	G	A	P	Pim
2002-03 CHI	13	1	1	2	31		DNQ			
2003-04 CHI	8	1	0	1	23		DNQ			
2005-06 CHI	10	0	0	0	16		DNQ			
2006-07 ANA	48	2	7	9	88	15	0	0	0	19
2007-08 BOS	58	4	3	7	74	7	0	0	0	6
2008-09 BOS	79	6	5	11	123	10	1	0	1	6
2009-10 BOS	74	1	9	10	141	12	0	0	0	4
2010-11 BOS	79	10	10	20	122	for 2011 playoff stats see p. 18				
NHL Totals	369	25	35	60	618					

for 2011 playoff stats see p. 18

Acknowledgements

The author would like to thank the many people involved in getting this book done with the utmost haste and care, starting with M & S president and publisher Doug Pepper and Jordan Fenn, publisher of the Fenn/M & S imprint, for their enthusiasm and support. Also to the editorial team at M & S, namely Liz Kribs, Michael Melgaard, Janine Laporte, and Ruta Liormonas. As well, to the designers at First Image, Michael Gray and Rob Scanlan, for taking the rough material and images and turning it into a good-lookin' book worthy of the event. To my agent Dean Cooke and his astounding assistant, Mary Hu, for sorting the business side of things out in an orderly manner. To the people at Donnelley's for a speedy turnaround from files to finished product, and to the always helpful staff at Getty, in particular Wilfred Tenaillon, Paul Michinard, Bruce Bennett, and Glenn Levy. And lastly to my personal team away from the ice—Liz, Ian, Zac, Emily, me mum, and meine frau, who just might live with me some day.